In life, we meet only a handl
human beings who have an
lives—people who display a.
with positivity and passion; the kind you could listen to for days
and still want more. In my nearly thirty years of speaking and con-
sulting millions of people around the globe, Vince Lee is one of
those rare people. His life speaks volumes to a life well lived, and
his words are well worth your attention.

Dale Vermillion
President and CEO
Vermillion Consulting/Mortgage Champions

Vince, you are always serving—*always*. You are an inspiration, and
I'm thankful I was able to get to know you and your wonderful
family at SMP. I love your hearts! With gratitude,

Tricia Migliazzo
Senior VP of Origination Sales
Lenders One

This book is such a gift, in which Vince is able to sum up the value
of what over twenty years of his mentorship has given me and
provide the rest of the world with a similar opportunity. With my
hard work and dedication, along with learning what Vince teaches, I am now Chief Legal Counsel of a growing IMB.

Madonna Blanchard, Esq.

Vince Lee, as both a superb communicator of his organization's corporate vision and a lifelong learner, inspires his team to maximize their potential. He has created an environment respectful of individual needs as well as accountability, a rare commodity in today's workforce.

Sue Scott
Leadership Performance Coach
Dale Carnegie Training, offered by Will Enterprises, Inc.

It is my pleasure to introduce the latest work of Vince Lee, my dear friend and mentor, who has been a leading figure in the real estate world for over five decades. This book is a culmination of his wealth of experience, insights, and wisdom gained through his long and successful career. Congratulations to Vince on this outstanding achievement!

Yasmine I. Poles
Circuit Court Judge

F U T U R E
MILLIONAIRES
AND HIGH ACHIEVERS

August 2024

Grace —

I hope that this book
can help you or someone
that you know.

Vince

FUTURE
MILLIONAIRES
AND HIGH ACHIEVERS

VINCE LEE

Future Millionaire and High Achievers
©2023 by Vince Lee

Published by Results Faster Publishing

Editing by Adept Content Solutions

Cover Design by Adept Content Solutions

Interior Design by Adept Content Solutions

Printed in the United States of America

Contents

"Never criticize,
condemn, or complain."
—Dale Carnegie

Dedication

This book is dedicated to all those who have the desire and discipline to put these principles to work, both in their life and business, and who become part of the rare millionaire club.

Purpose

*The book aims to share my life insights
from relationships to goals, setbacks, and achievements,
and help mortgage professionals determine whether
the positive family culture at Success Mortgage Partners
could better help them achieve their goals.*

Foreword

For over forty years I've been advising those at the very top to the next levels of results. That's what I do and who I am. I study everything, and that includes watching for special people to study—people who are different, exceptional, and have a proven track record of exceptional results. Vince Lee is one of those people.

About a year ago, one of my colleagues connected me to Success Mortgage Partners (SMP) and said, "These guys are like you, and I think you need to know them." So my team scheduled a Zoom call, which led to a powerful and inspirational call with Kevin Broughton, the executive VP at SMP. That call led to yet another powerful and inspirational call with Kevin's partner and SMP CEO, Owen Lee, which soon led me to their corporate office in Detroit.

When I visited for the first time, I was shown around and got to walk into an office I will forever remember. That office was Vince Lee's. When I walked in, I read inspirational messages on the wall that resonated with me; but what got me was a table—not just any table, but a table that was loaded with about ten book titles. Each title was stacked three to six or eight deep, so there were dozens of books. What I immediately recognized was that the owner of this office was like me. You see, I also keep extra copies of the best books that have impacted me in my office, ready to give away to those I meet. This guy, whom I had never met, was one of the few individuals who take the time to buy, store, and have ready to give away priceless wisdom. I was excited to one day meet this man, who is a partner to both Kevin and Owen and the cofounder of Success Mortgage Partners.

Their company eventually engaged me and my firm, and I was asked to keynote their annual event. I remember it like it was yesterday. Before my talk that morning, Vince spoke first for a good half hour. I was blown away. This eighty-seven-year-old man floored me with his message and impact. Within a very short time, I was asking him to please let my publishing company publish him. The book you have in your hands is the result.

We asked him to dig deep into his memory and craft a philosophy book based on what caused his massive success. This man has accumulated millions; attracted a very special wife of sixty-plus years; served a wonderful, loving family; and helped other people make millions—hence the title of the book, *Future Millionaires and High Achievers.*

What you're about to read is priceless. Please don't just read it. Study it, love it, and put the content to work for you, your team, and even your family. It can and will change your life forever! It's that good.

Vince and my great publishing team have gathered kernels of wisdom from his sixty-plus years of study, plus his stories, and aligned and organized them in such a way that they are readily digestible and easy to absorb.

Please make sure you send him a note or an e-mail once you read it. It will make his day. Tell him how you were impacted and what you're taking away that can help you win more. That's what his company is known for—**helping winners win more.**

Let me end with this one-liner exhortation: "Take advice only from those who have been there and done that or who are doing it now." Vince has been there and done it. He's a walking success story. Learn from both his failures and his successes. Be assured his stories are quite captivating—you won't want to put the book down.

Tony Jeary—The RESULTS Guy

TEN THINGS THIS BOOK WILL HELP YOU ACHIEVE:

1. Create a solid mindset base of positive thinking and the right beliefs

2. Develop a positive-thinking, beliefs, and goal-oriented leadership style

3. Sell from a position of Know, Like, and Trust

4. Find the ability to bounce back from difficult experiences and overcome obstacles

5. Increase your motivation and that of those around you

6. Help others win, and win yourself

7. Increase your positivity

8. Make you better at building relationships

9. Find the right knowledge sources to multiply success

10. Share smiles with those around you

Introduction

I am neither a scholar nor a scientist, nor was I ever even a great student. For me, getting out of grade school was no small feat.

When I was eleven, I had a sixth-grade teacher who told my parents I was a lovely boy. I behaved and didn't disrupt the class, but she couldn't morally pass me to the seventh grade because she wasn't sure I had the mental competency to do seventh-grade work. My mother was in shock; I have an older brother who had just skipped a grade because of his high intelligence.

After a moment of disbelief, my father told the teacher, "Nobody has more respect for teachers than me. I appreciate your experience, the challenges of the job, and the special interest and assistance you try to give my son Vincent. Unfortunately, his inability to do the sixth-grade work is partially my fault because I haven't had time to spend with him. I work for a company by the name of Special Engineering. We had a special assignment from the FBI. We were trying to improve the bombing sights on WWII bombers, because 80 percent of the bombs dropped on Germany were not hitting their targets. So effectively, by fixing the bomb sights, we could knock out the railroad tracks and the Germans couldn't move their supplies around as rapidly as our soldiers could advance. It saved lives. Now that the war has ended, the overtime has ended, and the urgency has ended, I have time to spend with Vincent in mathematics, reading, religion, science, and whatever it takes. If you pass Vincent, I'll put him in summer school and personally assist him in learning. By September, he'll be competent enough to do seventh-grade work." The teacher was so flattered that her jaw dropped, and she said she would pass me on my dad's promise of summer school and assistance.

Boy, was I happy when we left the room! As we walked down the hall, my mother was still in a state of shock, and I couldn't read the expression on my dad's face. We walked across the parking lot and got in the car. No one said anything until my dad parked the car at our house and turned the motor off. He said, "Vince, I got you out of the sixth grade. Get out of the seventh grade yourself." I never did go to summer school, or recieve additional help.

Although school wasn't my forte, I excelled at sales. When I went to Wayne State University, I met a lovely lady who was assessing students to shed light on what we should study and where our interests lay. After my evaluation, she walked into the room and asked, "Who's Vincent Lee?" And I said, "I am." She said, "I want to talk to you last; you're an odd duck." So, when she got to me, she said, "We can eliminate many occupations for you. We can eliminate accounting, engineering, music, and arts." I replied, "Well, that's interesting, but what do I do? Do I sell peanuts on the corner?" I'll never forget her response. I got positive feedback from a formal educator for the first time in my life. She remarked, "You fit in social work; real estate; stocks; financial advisor; minister, rabbi, or priest, depending on your denomination; as a civics history teacher in high school; or anything to do with human beings and family economic security. You could excel in any of those things."

I decided that real estate was the only thing that interested me and, at the time, I didn't own a home.

Much of my success has been from trial and error, books I have read, and relationships I have made. I wrote this book to give back and help shape others for success. I remember reading *How to Win Friends and Influence People* by Dale Carnegie. I realized that my problems, interactions, and aspirations were common. Everything I was going through had been experienced by others and was specifically addressed in Carnegie's book.

My hope is that through this book, as I lay out a guide to my beliefs and mindset, I can help make as many millionaires as possible. If you are already a millionaire, I hope to ensure you are getting the most that life can offer.

As Zig Ziglar said, "You can get anything in the world you want if you help enough people get what they want." I genuinely believe that, and it is something I live by. I have spent seven decades reading, learning, and living personal development. I have had ups and downs and learned a great deal. If I can live a happy and successful life, anyone can.

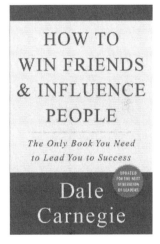

I've put together this book to dramatically impact your success. The content has been organized to help you digest it one bite at a time. The heart of the book includes ten critical areas of focus to help you become a millionaire. The first chapter, "Mindset," gives you the foundation for creating extraordinary success by changing your thoughts, examining what you believe, and adjusting accordingly. Chapter 2 is "Leadership." In Chapter 3 we talk about the concept of "Know, Like, and Trust." That chapter is followed by Chapter 4, "Resiliency," which shows you how to maximize your efforts as you put the formula to work—to survive and thrive. Then follows chapters on "Motivation," "Win-Win," and "Positivity" to help you utilize and enhance these attributes so you can become what everyone wants to be—a great leader, whether for your kids, your team members, or your entire company. Finally, the last chapters on "Relationships," "Knowledge," and "SMILE," teach you how to maximize those concepts, both personally and professionally, through standards, habits, and tools, and by putting together a team of people to help you.

I have also included highlights (below) from the ten chapters that can be used as a quick-start guide for those who want to understand the key messages quickly. You can either read the book from cover to cover or select the chapters most relevant to you.

Mindset

Key principle: Today's dream could be tomorrow's achievement. Nothing is accomplished without belief.

Leadership

Key principle: Leaders must believe, persuade, and have discipline and persistence.

Know, Like, and Trust

All three (know, like, and trust) must be present in a successful sale; two won't work.

Resiliency: Survive, Then Thrive

Key principle: Survive, then thrive.

Motivation

Key Principle: A clear goal with a realistic timetable is the tool that defeats inertia and overcomes obstacles.

Win-Win

Key principle: Responsible, good citizens usually enjoy better health and a happier, longer life because they resist resentment, retaliation, and reprisals, which are all negative in content and lead to negative thinking, negative action, and negative consequences.

Positivity

Key principle: Your altitude is determined by your attitude.

Relationships

Key Principle: Rich relationships create a rich life.

Knowledge

Key Principle: Education comes in many forms and knowledge is all around you. There is no "right" way to learn.

Smile

Key principle: A smile conveys friendship, acceptance, open-mindedness, and the fact that you are in a good mood.

FUTURE
MILLIONAIRES
AND HIGH ACHIEVERS

CHAPTER 1
MINDSET

Key Principle: Today's dream could be tomorrow's achievement. Nothing is accomplished without belief.

*"What you can conceive and believe,
you can achieve."*
—Napoleon Hill

Mindset, my first area of focus, is the foundation for the other nine. A solid base of positive thinking and the right beliefs prove to be a natural segue into developing the other traits necessary for success. You will become a leader who can persuade others to follow you because they know, like, and trust you. Your positive outlook, resiliency, and knowledge provide a high level of motivation, both for you and your team. In short, you become a winner who helps other people win, which is the formula for becoming a millionaire.

Positive Thinking

One of the constant, recurring themes in this book is positivity. It not only deserves an entire chapter in this book because of the benefits it brings, it also comprises a large part of the mindset concept.

I was in my early twenties when I read *The Power of Positive Thinking* by the Reverend Norman Vincent Peale.

It was terrific to me. People criticized Reverend Peale as a minister for telling people they could improve their life by positive thinking. He completely turned the tables on them. He said that as a minister, he had a moral responsibility to show people how to cut anxiety, worry, and stress from their life through positive thinking. When you read

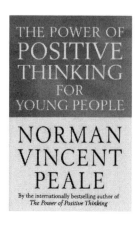

books like Dr. Joseph Murphy's *The Power of Your Subconscious Mind*, these ideas are confirmed.

With positive thinking, you live longer and live happier. When you reduce stress, you accomplish more.

When you have a goal, you have an image and a schedule, and you think positively. Anytime you think negatively, it creates an adverse reaction for your body. It increases stress. It takes time to protect productive advancement.

Your future is in your thoughts right now.

How you think and feel is what you accomplish. Why would you spend any time trying to be vindictive or trying to compare? You don't need to outsmart the other guy. What you have to do is improve yourself as a person and as a professional. I love positive-affirmation books, and it's great to read them, but you advance more if you apply them and don't just put them on the shelf. If you don't have time to read a book in one sitting, jump into that book, any part of it, for fifteen minutes a day. The attunement it brings gives you the competitive advantage to magnify and produce a recognized service that separates you from the competition, and it is excellent. The more that happens, the more your positive affirmation is identified in your subconscious mind, and the sooner what's in your subconscious mind ultimately becomes a reality.

Beliefs

There are many different ways to define belief: in your creative imagination, in the Bible, or in your motivation. In your creative vision, can you visualize an action taken or a feeling of accomplishment that doesn't exist now but could exist with your efforts? The Bible defines it simply as "as you believe"; it says, "All things are possible to him who believes" (Mark 9:23). The word *believe* is frequently used to motivate. Football coaches often say to their teams, "You have to believe we can win this game as a team." So, belief is when you visualize results that don't exist, when your logic and faith tell you they can and will live if you believe and take the necessary action. Belief is taking steps regardless of circumstances or overwhelming evidence that the goal is unrealistic. The mind cannot tell the difference between fact or fiction. It goes toward the dominant thought.

Let me repeat, there is great power in training your mind to focus on the positive, the belief that you can accomplish things. Doubt, negativity, and anxiety can be remedied by believing in your core that you can and will achieve your goal. A simple way to explain it is that many people have had some experiences in life, individual to them, where a parent, a teacher, an authority figure, an employer, or someone has told them they couldn't do a certain thing. However, because they had their definition, goal, or discipline, they made what the authority figure thought was impossible a reality.

Growing up, I had three older brothers with different talents. When you're the fourth child, regardless of what you accomplish, it's probably been achieved by your older siblings many times in your parents' eyes. So, I always tried to find something I believed I could do better than my older brothers. For example, I could swim better than my brothers, even before I had swimming lessons. I did the same thing in diving. I thought, *Height doesn't bother me, but it bothers my three older brothers*. With this belief, I became proficient on the diving board.

Later in life, I always believed I could succeed as a business-man. At the time, the big employers in Detroit were General Motors, Chrysler, and Ford, and they only wanted to hire you if you had a college degree. Now, I had been to college—for three years with two years of credits. However, I always believed I could gain more financial wealth than maybe 95 percent of people without studying what others learned. I was interested in a multitude of different topics including history, religion, and social work, but I believed that I was losing time and gaining nothing from going to college because too many courses were MANDATORY that I had little or no interest in. The mandatory core courses I was enrolled in didn't hold my attention. Then I was introduced to *The Strangest Secret* by Earl Nightingale.

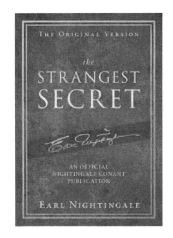

When we returned from our honeymoon, my wife and I had about $865 to our name. We rented an apartment for only $82 a month, and I drove an old used car. The Earl Nightingale record cost $19.50, but I told my wife it wasn't an expenditure of $19.50. It was an investment in our future. The book was just a story about the fact that the strangest secret is no secret. People can change their position in life by altering their minds. The mind will grow, cultivate, and make reality whatever you plant in it. If your thoughts are negative, you will yield negative experiences, and the same goes for the positive.

Regardless of what you're doing, what you're thinking, what your goals are, or what your situation is, if you alter your state of mind and start believing in something else, your circumstances will change, and you can leave to go where you want to go.

So, I thought *I might not fit in the college classroom, but I still fit in the business world.*

Most people work for money. Rich people have money work for them.

One day, I was driving and listening to the radio, and the radio interviewer talked to a man who was a prisoner of war in North Korea—an American soldier whose unit had been overrun. This man had lived longer than anyone else in the harsh circumstances in a North Korean prison camp. The radio host asked this soldier, "How did you do it? How did you survive when fellow prisoners and soldiers who were captured at the same time as you died?" He said, "It was not an artificial belief. I believed in my goal: to return to America, to my wife. Whatever the hardship was, I told myself, *I can put up with this because someday I'm going home.* I didn't put a schedule or a date on it. I saw so many fellow prisoners say to themselves, *I'm going to get out of here by Christmas time, or by my first or second or third anniversary of captivity, or by my birthday.* I think that was wrong. You can put a date on some goals, but not this one. Because I had no control over these events, I just promised myself that I would live to come home." After hearing the soldier's story, I said, *I must acknowledge that accomplishing my goals might take longer than I thought.*

In another instance, the US government came to Henry Ford and told him to stop making cars and begin building airplanes—six a day was the goal! Ford took the assignment, but he created a new production line rather than converting his original production line. President Roosevelt was frustrated with him because he was taking too much time. About twelve months later, Ford finished the new production line. By 1943 and 1944, Ford was turning out twenty-three planes a day—four times more than requested!

Every great visionary first has at his or her core a dream, a thought, or a belief that something that does not yet exist can exist. It is that belief that creates a driving force toward the impossible.

So, let's go back to Napoleon Hill's statement that "Whatever the mind can conceive and believe, it can achieve." I've read a quote from Henry Ford many times that says, "Whether you think you can or you can't, you're right."

"Whether you think you can or you can't, you're right." —Henry Ford

---

I have never had a limiting belief system. At some point in my life, I realized that nothing was unattainable and out of reach. There were dark days, sure, where at SMP we could barely afford a pizza or pay some of the bills coming in, but it was always essential to talk about the future, the promised land, and a common goal, nonstop. I refuse, to this day, to place any limitations on what is possible. I feel that limited belief systems are the most common things in the world, and they're the number one killer of successful life stories. They can stop anyone from going from where they are to where they say they want to be. I have never sent an e-mail that in any way, shape, or form contained a limiting belief statement. So again, the idea that "Whether you think you can or you can't, you're right" is an excellent lesson because it's 100 percent true.

Another great lesson I learned came out of the mouth of a cricket. You read that right—a cricket. Walt Disney was an incredible source of inspiration to me.

Growing up, he had a callous father and a difficult childhood. Now, Walt Disney knew kids wouldn't listen to a thirty-year-old like him, so he had a cricket do the speaking for him.

Disney believed you could be rich, poor, educated, or uneducated; it made no difference.

"When you wish upon a star...
It's like, if you have a dream,
when you wish upon a star, it makes
no difference who you are."
—Jiminy Cricket

From my point of view, the power of imagination can take you through your beliefs down the highway to success.

"If your heart is in your dream,
if your passion is in your head,
no request is too extreme."
—Jiminy Cricket

Goals

Along the same line, I am very passionate about goals. They are the roadmap to success. Be aggressive in your goal setting. Ensure you create and aspire to big, worthwhile, audacious goals. When you have a goal, put a "+" at the end of it so that you never limit yourself.

My goals are frequently lofty, and sometimes people ask, "Is this guy crazy?" It's not craziness; it's just me, consumed with passion, purpose, and belief. I believe in having goals, writing them down, and announcing some of them to the world. Be bold and tell people what your goals are. I've told the members of my company that I want to make money, and I've said, "I'll help any person in this company achieve any level of success they want as long as they don't impede my ability to be successful as well." It isn't a place of selfishness or greed. I really do want to make as many people as financially successful as possible. But it's also essential to remain focused on your own pursuit of success. It's okay if your goals are big and seem impossible so long as you have them. Write them down and tell them to someone.

Success has been defined as the progressive realization of a worthwhile, predetermined goal. After reading many success books, I found a definition I feel more comfortable with: "Success is getting what you want in life without walking on someone else's toes." That philosophy is beneficial in encouraging culture as well. Remember Zig Ziglar's words about success: "You can obtain anything in life you want as long as you help enough people get what they want." So, the key to achieving your goals is having a positive image of yourself, which you can only have if you're doing the right thing in the right way.

Mindset Vince-isms

1. Embrace a growth mindset: Adopting a growth mindset means seeing failures and setbacks as opportunities to learn and grow. You believe that your skills and abilities can be developed through dedication and hard work rather than just innate talent.

2. Take action: Success doesn't come from just thinking about it; it comes from taking action. Create a plan, set achievable goals, and take consistent steps toward them.

3. Learn from failure: Instead of dwelling on failures and setbacks, use them as opportunities to learn and grow. Analyze what went wrong, identify the lessons learned, and use that knowledge to do better next time.

4. Stay persistent: Success takes time and effort. Stay persistent and keep working toward your goals, even when it's tough. Remember that setbacks and failures are a natural part of the journey, and keep pushing forward.

CHAPTER 2
LEADERSHIP

Key Principle: Leaders must believe, persuade, and have discipline and persistence.

"Success is the ability to go from one failure to another, with no loss of enthusiasm."
—Winston Churchill

A strong understanding of Mindset is essential to being a strong leader. When you lead with positive-thinking, solid and authentic beliefs, and worthwhile goals, you become the kind of person others will want to follow. Like attracts like, thoughts are things, and attitudes are contagious, so you need to have an enthusiastic attitude of gratitude and *be able to express it* to lead the right way.

Leadership is "leading a group of people or an organization and working towards a common goal." My definition of a leader is someone who, through a cooperative spirit and positive interaction, can get a group to willingly believe in and work toward a worthwhile, predetermined goal. When you maintain a positive and limitless belief system, you can achieve goals that some would think are unimaginable. When you can also get other people to believe it's a worthy cause and that they can contribute to it, you can achieve the unthinkable together.

What's a Leader?

Historically, Winston Churchill is considered by many people to be one of the greatest and most influential leaders of the twentieth century, even though he failed the sixth grade! At a time when it looked like Germany was about to take over all of Europe, he was thrust into both the power and responsibility of leadership for an entire nation when he was named the prime minister of England. Given the job largely because no one else wanted it, this man, looked down upon by many of his peers, was the only thing standing between the Nazis and Western Europe. Germany had invaded and occupied many European countries before Churchill was named prime minister. On the day he took office, Germany launched invasions into France, Holland, and Belgium. England was directly in their sights, but Churchill had *belief*. The thought of surrender was impossible for him to imagine, and he focused all his energies on survival and victory.

> ## "Let us, therefore, brace ourselves to our duties, and so bear ourselves that, if the British Empire and its Commonwealth last for a thousand years, men will still say, 'This was their finest hour.'"
> ## —Winston Churchill

As Napoleon Hill said, what the mind can conceive, it can believe and achieve. Churchill could envision victory over Germany, which allowed him to believe in the possibility of it, and ultimately, he helped lead England to achieve it. There were plenty of setbacks along the way, as success comes with failure, but he persevered from one failure to the next with no loss of enthusiasm, no loss of conviction, and no loss of his belief. Churchill believed so strongly that they could defeat Germany that he convinced and persuaded an entire nation that it would be better to die than surrender to such an abusive enemy. He had a genuine belief, a worthwhile, identifiable, and predetermined goal that England could be victorious.

When I was ten years old, I was reading a story in the local Detroit newspaper. The Second World War was ongoing then, and this article struck me about leadership and how they identify leaders in foxholes. This GI was talking about how when you're in a foxhole surrounded by the enemy, the survival and success of the group depend upon the actions of every individual. You don't want to be in the foxhole to the north only to find out the guy protecting the western flank to your side has deserted and surrendered to the enemy while you're still trying to fight. Everyone needs to be in it together.

So, in all events, it's crucial that the leader get the group to have an authentic belief in their goal, that they can display and convey confidence in accomplishing that goal, and that they can identify those within the group who don't want to buy into the objective you're trying to accomplish. If someone in the group isn't truly behind it, he or she must find a new group and goal. Any worthwhile movement in the history of human beings, whether it's a military goal, a production goal, a religious goal, or a social or business goal, has involved leadership that displayed confidence, inspiration, and determination in their belief to accomplish their goal with those around them.

Even kids learn to recognize a leader. I was in the fifth grade the first time I realized I might have some natural leadership qualities, and this was a pivotal moment in my life. As I said before, I wasn't the best student growing up, but as far as I can remember, I have always had a natural ability to make friends. People usually liked me, and I liked people. So, one day before recess, my fifth-grade teacher gathered the class together and split us into three different groups; a row of boys, a row of girls, and another row of boys and girls.

"Kids," she said, "I've split you into teams so that you can play baseball with each other outside. Now, I need a leader for each team. This leader has to be fair and honest and has to be able to explain, inspire, take charge, and be tolerant." There were six of us in each group, and she wanted us to vote for whom we wanted the team leader to be. I felt lucky because I got five out of six votes!

She was about to hand me the glove with the ball in it, but then she held back. "No," she said, "Let's do this again. You need to vote for a fair and honest leader who can explain and inspire, takes charge, is tolerant, and most importantly, is a good student!" She thought this might eliminate me. The second time around, I got four out of six votes, so I only lost one vote, and I still got to be the team leader! I thought, "Wow, some students think I'm a leader." This was the first time I had experienced anything like this, being recognized by my peers as a leader. It was a profound experience and an excellent early lesson in life leadership. The teacher might not have thought I was the best team leader, but the team thought I was. Getting the buy-in, support, and cooperation of the group is essential and plays true in all areas of leadership you might find yourself in.

Another time, I was in the seventh grade, and a group of friends and I were playing football in the street. We played two-hand touch, and the teams were equally matched, so everyone had a good time. We were running up and down the street until, all of a sudden, there was a play that disrupted the game. The opposing team had a catch and run that they thought should be a touchdown, but everyone on my team felt the receiver had been tagged down with both hands before scoring. They were all very loud and excited about the situation, while I stayed calm and collected, just watching, not jumping to voice an opinion one way or the other.

They started getting animated in their arguments until, finally, my cousin, who was the oldest person in the game, looked at me and said, "Vince, do you think the guy scored a touchdown or not?" I looked back at him and said, "I know I'm not on their team, but I think he scored." And just like that, everyone accepted it and the game immediately moved on! Now, I don't know why everybody was willing to accept my opinion so quickly, but I do know that I was among a group of people that both knew and liked me and that I was being honest with my belief and opinion. My team trusted me to be fair and was willing to be persuaded by what I thought.

Be a trusted leader, follow through, and do what you say you will do.

Every Group Needs a Leader

Any group looking to achieve something together needs a leader, or the mission or goal will never be accomplished. It's pretty profound when you think about it.

I think people can generally identify who the leader is just by being around them and taking notice. We start learning this practice as early as preschool because even children know how to play follow the leader. I say this to point out that leadership can come in all shapes, sizes, and colors. Young or old, rich or poor, new or experienced, **what remains constant in good leaders is that they have a rich and robust self-belief, can persuade those around them, are disciplined, and are persistent in pursuit of achieving their goals**. All you need to do is look to history to see the wide range of people who have proven themselves to be tremendous leaders. Believe in yourself, become persuasive, and be disciplined and persistent, pursuing your goals.

When I think of someone like Joan of Arc, it reminds me that some leaders achieved accomplishments that truly defy imagination and belief. Now a patron saint of France, she grew up as a peasant on a farm and went on to lead the nation's army when she was seventeen years old during the Hundred Years' War. Just think of that: a seventeen-year-old woman leading armies of men into battle, fighting back and defeating the English, and inspiring an entire nation of people to rally to her cause. It is such an awe-inspiring piece of history. Here in the United States, John F. Kennedy was elected to be the youngest president in the history of our country in 1961 at just forty-three years old. He, too, inspired a nation.

"Hope renewed, goals obtained, dreams fulfilled."
—Vince Lee

He led America through the space race; the Cold War; a national economic, social, and political struggle for equality; and the Cuban missile crisis. Working with other historical leaders like Dr. Martin Luther King, President Kennedy helped the Civil Rights movement in the United States in ways that many probably thought inconceivable at the time. Dr. King and President Kennedy were great speakers, with a fantastic ability to convey their beliefs and goals to a group of people, persuade others in favor of their cause, and persist in the face of overwhelming adversity from oppositional forces. I think any great leader can take on an unpopular cause, provided it is one they truly believe in. It's the authenticity and belief in it that matters. The most shining examples of this that I can think of are Jackie Robinson and Jesse Owens. These two athletes suffered inhuman abuse and hatred while displaying magnificent confidence and restraint. While Jackie Robinson was breaking the color barrier in Major League Baseball, he was restricted from sharing facilities and showering with the team, forced to use different entrances, and racially taunted and abused everywhere he went. He would receive death threats daily, but his belief and confidence in himself and his cause far outweighed the hatred and abuse he endured.

"Americans are a strange people. You can lead them with a lollipop, but you cannot push them with a bayonet." —Winston Churchill

---

Recognition and Appreciation

Never in the history of our civilization has a general commanding an army on behalf of a nation won a battle by talking negatively to their troops. Can you imagine? If a leader was to tell his troops, "The enemy is on the horizon, they have better intelligence and equipment than we do, more advantageous terrain, they outnumber us three to one, and we'll probably all be dead by tomorrow at noon," that leader would be standing alone by sunrise because all his troops would have deserted! It's just a basic fact that if you speak negatively and negatively carry yourself in front of your team, they will pick up on it. You must instill the good and the positive in what you are trying to accomplish. If the leader is negative, that negativity will exponentially spread throughout your group or team. Never forget the power of positive thought and how by shifting and countering negative thoughts with positive ones you can reduce stress, doubt, worry, and anxiety on yourself and those around you whom you intend to lead.

I sometimes like to think of myself as a farmer in the business world. At Success Mortgage Partners, I'll even jest occasionally that I'm in charge of the Department of Sunshine and Rainbows!

Never complete a negative thought. Always counter it with a positive one.

I say that because by planting seeds of praise, appreciation, and positive thought in the minds of those around me, I must continue to water those seeds with more of the same and watch the growth increase. That growth is then amplified and multiplied when it spreads throughout the culture of your team. When you lead this way, I believe it promotes the reduction of stress on your team or company, it allows them to be more efficient in their work toward the realization of your common goal, and this ultimately allows everyone to save time and work more efficiently. Who among us doesn't wish we had more time?

I always like to do it indirectly when it is required to call attention to people's mistakes. Typically, I like to lead with my own mistakes. This conveys to whomever you're speaking with that you're humble, self-aware, and understand that everyone makes mistakes. Then, I like to offer a "criticism sandwich." The ingredients are a compliment, followed by the constructive criticism you must provide, and finished with another compliment. This allows the other person to save face and discourages a naturally defensive position he or she might take. Following any constructive criticism, I believe it's important to praise even the slightest improvement and then continue to praise every improvement after that.

I've hired many people over sixty-plus years in the real estate business, and no one has ever come to me and said, "Vince, the reason I'm leaving my existing employer is that they appreciate me too much and communicate with me too much." Hundreds of times, I have heard it the other way around—no appreciation, no communication. **Knowing this, leading your team should always begin with an approach of praise, communication,**

You don't plant an apple seed and sprout an orange tree.

and honest appreciation. Mistakes will be made, and challenges will always present themselves. However, you will never earn the right to be constructively critical of someone on your team without having an honest appreciation for them.

We are all human beings, and no matter what race, religion, ethnicity, or nationality, we all have things in common. One of the strongest things is the human need to be recognized and appreciated. I remember when I was in my early twenties, I was walking by a TV, and an interview was playing over the air that caught my attention. The interviewer was speaking to Mrs. Dorothy Carnegie, the widow of Dale Carnegie. They discussed some of his experiences with the Dale Carnegie courses, and the topic of appreciation came up.

They went back and forth shortly before, almost frustratingly, the interviewer interjected, "I'm sorry, Mrs. Carnegie, but I remember the leadership chapter very clearly, ma'am," he said, "and learned about the benefits and positive effects of recognition and appreciation."

"No, sir," said Mrs Carnegie. "Reread it, sir. Dale never taught in the leadership course the benefits or positive effects of recognition and appreciation. He taught us how we, as human beings, *crave* recognition and appreciation. We crave it, sir."

So, if you want to lead successfully and excel professionally, showing honest appreciation and recognition is something you should do. *Honest* is the key word because everybody knows the difference between insincere flattery and authentic recognition and appreciation. True and honest appreciation reinforces a positive affirmation in the team member's mind; it creates a win-win situation, and everyone involved benefits.

"Efficiency is doing things right; effectiveness is doing the right things."
—Henry Ford

Lead by Example

There was a time early on in my business career when I was a Century 21 broker, and I was running my real estate sales office in Michigan. We opened at 9 am, and I always tried to get in around 8 am or so, just to make sure things were running right. Whether it was making sure the lights worked, or that the office was clean and orderly, or maybe that I needed to coordinate with team members who were calling in sick, or whether there was anything else that might have come up, there were always things that could be done to make sure we could get through the day more efficiently and effectively. As the team leader, I felt I was responsible for doing everything I could be to ensure the office was functioning correctly, running smoothly, and maintaining a professional appearance. So, I pulled into the parking lot one morning, and after I parked, I noticed another car in the lot. When I got my keys in the lock, the gentleman from that car had walked up and said, "You must be the guy I want to see; you're Vincent Lee, right?"

"Yes," I said, "I'm Vince, and who are you?" He was a local newspaper salesperson selling advertising to real estate brokers. "How did you know I'm Vincent Lee?" I asked. The man said, "Because my records show you're the broker here, sir, and I've been doing this for a long time. Who else but the owner would be the first one here, reaching in the bushes to pick up the two empty beer cans and throwing them away!" He said, "So you must be the owner because you understand that image and efficiency are important. You're the first person here to see that the place will be running well today, and you're picking up the empty beer cans because you know that first impressions are important." It's a funny story to me, but it does help illustrate how successful leadership requires that you lead by example and look to create and improve efficiencies for your team whenever and wherever you can.

Being effective and efficient as a leader should always be at the forefront of your mind. By creating and increasing efficiencies, you save your team time, which as I discussed earlier, helps to reduce stress, doubt, worry, and anxiety. Most of the time, it can even save you some money too! Henry Ford was a master at improving efficiencies and effectiveness in his manufacturing process. Before Ford's manufacturing revolution, the workers went to work, there were inefficiencies up and down the line, and the production was solely dependent upon the ability of the skilled craftsman. It took twelve long hours to produce a single vehicle. Ford *believed* he could do things better.

Ford developed four main principles to increase efficiency and effectiveness in his production: interchangeable and replaceable parts, a perpetual workflow, division of labor, and reduced wasted power and effort. No longer would the workers be going to work; now the work would be going to the workers. With the creation of the assembly line, he was able to decrease the production time of a vehicle by almost 90 percent. What once took twelve hours to complete could now be done in 90 minutes! By using interchangeable and replaceable parts, he improved the workflow, decreased shift hours for his employees, paid his employees more, and reduced the cost of his product. Ford's leadership approach and *belief* that he could create and improve efficiencies resulted in tremendous benefits to his company, his workers, and his customers.

What good is a leader who never receives a challenge?

Leadership Vince-isms

- Communication: A great leader is an excellent communicator. Communication is key to effectively delegating tasks, providing feedback, and inspiring a team to work toward a common goal. Effective communication also involves being an active listener and understanding the needs and concerns of team members.

- Lead by example: Great leaders lead by example. They set the standard for their team by demonstrating a strong work ethic, a positive attitude, and a commitment to achieving goals. When leaders model the behavior they expect from their team, it inspires them to do the same.

- Develop your team: Great leaders focus on developing their team members. They invest time and resources into their professional growth and provide opportunities for them to learn new skills and take on new challenges. Leaders who prioritize the development of their team build a more skilled and motivated workforce.

- Build trust: Trust is an essential component of effective leadership. Leaders who build trust with their team members create a positive and productive work environment. Trust is built through consistent actions, transparency, and honest communication.

- Empower your team: Empowering team members means giving them the autonomy to make decisions and take ownership of their work. When team members feel empowered, they are more motivated and invested in their work.

CHAPTER 3
KNOW, LIKE, AND TRUST

Key Principle: All three (know, like, and trust) must be present in a successful sale; two won't work.

If you don't have integrity, you have nothing.
—Henry Kravis

Here's an important thing everyone should know: When buying a home, automobile, or mortgage, we've all experienced misrepresentation or being talked down to, and we've often not purchased the product. Now, analyze that and intentionally choose to take the opposite approach. Everyone needs products, and everyone starts as a rookie. No one wants to look or feel stupid, and we usually like to work with similar people with specific knowledge. If you're looking to sell, the easiest way is to find someone with a need and convey the product to them in a way they relate to (Know, Like, Trust) that fits their needs and budget.

People like people who accept them. Often, you don't accept people until you get to know them, and when you build a relationship over time you create mutual trust. People usually have an innate feeling of whom they can trust. And when you trust somebody, you don't second guess them or spend time figuring out why they said this or did that. From that point of view, unless you have a reason not to, you ought to initially interact with new people from a high position of know, like, and trust. Your eyes, voice, facial features, handshake, and body language convey messages to people. Some say people decide whether they will like you in the first fifteen, thirty, forty-five, or fifty-five seconds.

When you have that trifecta of know, like, trust and rapport with others, you become known as a person of integrity.

Intentionally embracing a know, like, and trust mindset is crucial to facilitating a successful work and life environment.

Know

As a general rule, we like knowledgeable people. That is, of course, as long as they aren't arrogant know-it-alls. There's a big difference between talking with someone who can speak intelligently about a subject and someone determined to prove they are more intelligent than everyone else. Appearing knowledgeable is not about pretending to know everything but about demonstrating confidence and competence in your expertise. When selling anything (even your ideas) to an individual, it is important to remember that establishing rapport is more important than showing all of your knowledge. Most of us have experienced an overly enthusiastic salesperson. It's pretty hard to build a connection with someone if you can't get a word in edgewise. Ensure that you read your client before you present to them. Determine what's important to them and tailor your presentation to highlight those areas of the product or service, rather than overloading them with information.

Here are some Vince-isms on how to be knowledgeable while selling:

- Be humble: Humility is an important quality to have when sharing your knowledge with others. Acknowledge that you don't know everything and are open to learning from others.

- Share your knowledge selectively: Be mindful of the appropriate time and place to share your knowledge. Only interject during conversations if you have something valuable to contribute.

- Listen actively: Be an active listener when others are speaking. Show interest in what they have to say and ask thoughtful questions. This helps build rapport and establish mutual respect.

- Be respectful: Respect others' opinions and perspectives, even if you disagree with them. Avoid belittling or dismissing others' ideas, which can be arrogant and disrespectful.

- Stay curious: Keep an open mind about the world around you. This can help you to continue learning and growing while also staying grounded.

Remember that being knowledgeable is not about showing off or proving yourself to be better than others. It's about sharing your insights and expertise in a helpful and respectful way to others. By being respectful and curious, you can quickly establish a sales rapport and a win-win!

Like

Relationship-oriented sellers prioritize their connection with the customer over all other aspects of the sale. When people like someone, they feel that the person understands their needs and preferences. This can lead to a more personalized and tailored sales experience, which is typically more appealing to clients.

People like those who do the following:

- Inspire you or make you see things in a new light
- Share similar values
- Display positivity

To increase your likability, provide real value in your content, not a sales spiel. It also helps to demonstrate your unique personality

---

"Stop selling. Start helping."
—Zig Ziglar

---

and style. Do you express your company culture? Read your client and tap into the ideal situation within their imagination. Liking comes down to being open and honest and being who you are. Be open about your skills and values and how they can benefit your client (not sell to them).

TIP: A common interest is the success of the people you serve. Don't forget to ask them about their story.

Trust

Trust is essential to any successful business or relationship. Building consumer trust, especially on high-ticket sales, can be difficult. Consumers want to feel safe in their purchase and be reassured that you and your product are the right choices for their lifestyle. Trust stems from integrity. If you're known in your industry as a person of integrity, your opinions are more likely to matter, despite a lack of formal education or anything else. You'll exude a *vibe* that customers will pick up on. Further, if you do it right, your internal compass will be so strong that it shapes others around you, leading to a better team overall.

Below are a few Vince-isms for building trust:

- Provide social proof: Share testimonials from people who have consumed your products or services.

- Share stories of how you successfully helped others achieve results.

- Be transparent: Let people see who and what you are—and who and what you're not.

Everyone wants to purchase a product or a service from someone they know, like, and trust.

- Be accessible: Place your contact details on every piece of promotional material. From the prospect's perspective, it's nice to be on someone's site and see that they can be easily reached.

I once walked by one of my salespeople being interrupted by the client's friends while he was getting a purchase agreement signed. That's typically the worst time to stop in and socialize with somebody, because it's a high-pressure moment of trust and accountability. In the midst of the deal, the client's friends said, "Oh my God, it's a quarter to two, we promised to be on the golf course at a certain time. Let's go and continue this later." Rather than being annoyed at the interruption or letting the client go, the salesperson said, "Wait, I want to be on the golf course too. But because we're all friends and we want to remain friends, let's just take another five minutes to write and sign the agreement while it's clear in everyone's mind." When I heard that, I thought, *Wow, everybody should teach this*. This transaction, and the way the salesperson handled it, was the perfect embodiment of the principles of Know, Like, and Trust. Rather than being flustered and trying to show off his knowledge to the newcomers, he remained humble and allowed them to speak during the transaction. He also placed trust in his friendship and ensured that all parties felt respected, resulting in a win for everyone. He stated that their friendship was important and he wanted to keep it. He further suggested they finish the job they started and put the details on paper while they all agreed to the terms and contract. This helped preserve their friendship.

Know, Like, and Trust Vince-isms

- Be humble: Humility is an important quality to have when sharing your knowledge with others. Acknowledge that you don't know everything and be open to learning from others.

- Share your knowledge selectively: Be mindful of the appropriate time and place to share your knowledge. Only interject during conversations if you have something valuable to contribute.

- Listen actively: Be an active listener when others are speaking. Show interest in what they have to say and ask thoughtful questions. This helps build rapport and establish mutual respect.

- Be respectful: Respect others' opinions and perspectives even if you disagree with them. Avoid belittling or dismissing others' ideas, which can be arrogant and disrespectful.

- Stay curious: Keep an open mind about the world around you. This can help you to continue learning and growing while also staying humble.

- Provide social proof: Share testimonials from people who have consumed your products or services. Share stories of how you successfully helped others achieve results.

- Be transparent: Let people see who and what you are—and who and what you're not.

- Be accessible: Place your contact details on every conspicuous possible place you can. From the prospect's perspective, it's nice to be on someone's site and see that you can reach them easily.

CHAPTER 4
RESILIENCY

Key Principle: Survive, then thrive

"Failure is a detour, not a dead-end street."
—Zig Ziglar

P rize fighters are not usually quoted in relation to success, motivation, or successful action. However, Rocky Marciano, the only undefeated heavyweight champion in boxing history, spent a good portion of his life being told many discouraging things, such as he'd never make it as a professional boxer, or as a baseball player, or that he had no job skills. He suffered from unforgivable dimensions (a stocky 5'10", 185-pound frame, and his 67-inch reach was the shortest of any heavyweight champion). Yet he overcame it all to become a legendary figure in the ring. His 49-0 record still stands today as a hallmark to his enduring legacy. When asked how many times he got knocked down in his career, he avoided the question. When the question was repeated, he answered: "I don't know, and even if I did, it's not important." He said, "I don't keep track of how many times I got knocked down in a fight. The only thing that matters is that I got back up and finished the fight every time I got knocked down." This advice rings true for anybody in the business world, not just the boxing ring. It doesn't matter if you get knocked down as long as you get up with a positive attitude, analyze why you got knocked down, and use it as a steppingstone to further success.

Resiliency might be the fourth of the ten key principles, but it is undoubtedly one of the most important. Without the ability to bounce back from difficult experiences and overcome obstacles that come your way, it is near impossible to find high levels of success. Intentionally cultivating resiliency is key to finding inner strength and the determination to keep going, even when things get tough. Over the years, people have told me that I've been a success. While this may be true, I've also made many errors. I fell into a lot of potholes, but I believe that it doesn't really matter. It makes you a better businessman if you get up every time, analyze why you made a mistake, and proactively put into practice rules, decisions, and guidelines on how to avoid that type of error in the future. The only thing worse than bad news is bad news delayed.

If you intentionally program your mind that you're going to get up after every setback, it reinstalls confidence. I believe that you then speak not with cockiness but with more confidence. The right people see that for what it is, and it attracts positive people to you.

> ## *"F-E-A-R has two meanings: 'Forget Everything And Run' or 'Face Everything And Rise.' The choice is yours."*
> ## —Zig Ziglar

As you probably know, the only thing permanent is change. Everybody goes through life with some successes and some adversities. Properly dealt with, you could say these are just stepping stones on a ladder to success. Tony Jeary states that life is a series of presentations. I also believe a successful life, in business and personally, is a series of overcoming adversities.

When I was in my early thirties, I left the real estate broker I was selling with and started my own company. It took me about three years to get up to eight salespeople. I was working long hours, appraising and selling real estate, managing the office, and recruiting, until the company could be self-sufficient and pay its own bills. Then one day, seven of my eight salespeople informed me that they were quitting. A competitor down the street had offered to pay them more money via a higher sales commission. I couldn't afford to meet it, so seven of the eight people left; one stayed with me. I was set back three years of effort. Within less than six months, the competitor that stole my sales force went out of business. As it would happen, six of the seven people who left offered to come back. I was determined to start anew with a new group of people who believed in me more. Having overcome and lived through it, I was able to rebuild my sales force to twenty-two people in a different location. Afterwards, I took time to reflect on what I learned and used that knowledge to improve my business moving forward. That experience was pivotal in giving me the confidence level I needed to overcome any future business adversity. Warren Buffet says it's okay when you go into business with a person who's been bankrupt at least once. You learn a lot about resiliency from bankruptcy. You can learn so much more about yourself, your team, and your limits when faced with adversity. Learning from our mistakes and adversities and having the strength to put ourselves back together make us stronger and more well-rounded individuals.

One of the other pivotal resiliency moments in my life occurred years after my wife and I married. We'd gotten married at twenty-four, and at that age, most young newlyweds have a baby within a year or two. My wife and I had no success in getting pregnant for over seven years. My wife was very discouraged. We had both been to a series of physicians to try to overcome any adversities in sperm count or sperm life. And because I believe in being a long-range problem solver in my thinking, I wrote to all of the medical fertility departments of twenty major universities in the United States and included the results that my wife and I had after seeing a series of doctors over seven years.

Go as far as you can see, and then you can see further.

My wife was impressed with this determination. Being in the education profession as a teacher and having belief in medical universities and the prestigious ones I had written to, she was willing to give it a chance to see the results. I had very little encouragement and almost no response, until I was sitting at my desk doing an appraisal report one day when I had a call from a doctor who introduced himself as being in charge of the medical fertility and infertility department at Harvard University. After introducing himself, he explained that he didn't really understand the situation. In response, I tried to tactfully point out that I sent him all the medical knowledge and results I had. Listening patiently, the doctor asked, "Have you talked to Dr. Kamran Moghissi? He's the most knowledgeable medical doctor in the United States on matters of fertility and infertility, in my opinion. He teaches at Wayne State University in Detroit, and when he has a class on the subject, the rest of us get on an airplane flying to Detroit to learn." I explained that I was a student and that I would call Dr. Moghissi right away. When I called his office, his wife, acting as his assistant, answered the phone. We set up an appointment. He didn't rely on other medical reports, and he started building our new medical file. Within about eight months, my wife was pregnant.

The moral of the story is that in my early twenties, I was already a student and believer that so-called adversities can be overcome. Solutions are in the universe; and if you persistently pursue for the answers, somebody with knowledge will be ready to share that knowledge. This mentality, as well as Dr. Moghissi's expertise, contributed to the success of my daughter's being born and our having a son approximately three years later. Net result: I believe the only person who fails is the person who fails to try.

The only person who fails is the person who fails to keep trying. Success is a word with many different definitions. Some people define success in academic terms, athletic successes, business successes, success in raising a family or financial success, and so on.

The road to success is seldom, if ever, a straight line. It usually has many road blocks or detours, and frequently the road exists without adequate street signs.

Because of these facts, frequently success, however you define it, is a matter of many adjustments, changes in location, products, services, employees, and so on. You could have good products or services in the wrong location, or you could have a good location with the wrong products or services. Market economies, local or national, could be temporarily against you.

Lack of success does not mean that you failed, it could mean you just have not yet received the rewards that you should receive in proportion to your talent, energy, time, money invested, and so on.

Adjustments could be needed in any of the situations mentioned above. The true goal that you are pursuing may need to be redirected into a more appropriate obtainable goal that better fits your time, talent, money invested, professional skills, and so on.

From start to accomplishment, many adjustments are needed in any business venture. Setbacks and adjustments in location, occupation, market, services, and products are frequently needed.

My primary advice would be to reassure you that if success, as you define it, has not yet been reached, you have not failed. You may just need to reorganize your goals on your road to success as you define success.

Final statement: My experience tells me that the best advice that I can give you is to never lose faith in yourself.

Resiliency Vince-isms

- Build a support team: Having a strong support network of family, friends, or colleagues can help you through difficult times. Reach out to trusted individuals when you need support or advice.

- Focus on the present: It's easy to get caught up in worrying about the future or concentrating on past mistakes. However, focusing on the present moment can help you build resiliency by reducing stress and anxiety.

- Practice gratitude: Cultivating a sense of gratitude can help shift your focus from negative to positive. Taking time to appreciate the good things in your life can help you maintain a positive outlook, even during challenging times.

- Learn from setbacks: Resilient individuals view setbacks and failures as opportunities for growth and learning. Reflecting on what went wrong and what you can do differently next time can help you build resiliency and improve your chances of success in the future.

- Stay optimistic: Maintaining a positive outlook can help you build resiliency by keeping you motivated and hopeful, even in the face of adversity. Instead of focusing on what could go wrong, focus on the opportunities and possibilities that exist.

CHAPTER 5

MOTIVATION

Key Principle: A clear goal with a realistic timetable is the tool that defeats inertia and overcomes obstacles.

*"Remembering your positive action today
and overcoming today's obstacles leads you
to accomplish your dreams of tomorrow."*
—Vince Lee

Motivation is a crucial indicator of success. Now, I'm not just talking about general goals and beliefs; I'm talking about the motivation to get started and to keep going. There will always be reasons not to start, continue, or finish, and there are always a few people who don't want to see you succeed. Do you surround yourself with people who motivate you? Staying motivated over the long term can be challenging, but it's possible with the right strategies. I highly recommend regularly reflecting and celebrating your wins, no matter how small. You might also find an accountability partner to help you on your journey. Above all, always remember to care for yourself and know your limits. Sometimes the best motivation is to step back and come back fresh.

Personal Motivation

Before you can begin to motivate those around you, you must first learn what motivates you. One of the things I hear most often is,

"Vince, you're always so motivated! What's your secret?" And honestly, I am motivated—I've been motivated all my life. Motivation and momentum are two sides to the same coin for high achievers because you can motivate yourself, and you can also motivate the people around you to help them succeed as well. That leads to a much more significant result than most leaders can achieve individually.

When Success Mortgage Partners was a new company twenty years ago, our entire team went into the basement for a good review planning session. At this point, we didn't have any fancy projectors for meetings; we just had a tear-away flip chart. After a few hours, we had vision boarded the whole company, all laid out on twelve huge wall pads. We didn't have anything but a business card. We didn't have one flier; we didn't have one website; we didn't have one employee; we didn't have anything but the vision of what we would become.

Setting goals is essential to staying motivated because it gives you a clear direction and purpose to work toward. With goals, it can be easier to stay focused and motivated because you need a specific target to aim for. Having a clear goal in mind provides you with a sense of purpose and gives you something to strive toward, which can help you stay motivated.

Growing up as the fourth of five siblings, all boys, my initial motivation stemmed from fear. I feared not being recognized as equal in intelligence, ability, or effort. My siblings excelled at something, and all were good at most things. Whenever I accomplished something, it usually had already been done by one of my brothers. As a result, I wasn't too tuned in for most things. Once in a while though, I tuned in at school when the teacher talked about history, geography, and religion. I learned these topics quickly; I could learn as fast as anybody else in the class. My desire to learn motivated me when I was young, because I saw one place where I could excel. My other brothers didn't care much about history or geography. I set a goal to excel in those areas.

When I was very young, I was motivated by a desire for independence. I drew pictures to sell for ten cents to buy a popsicle without going to my mother or dad for money. Later, when I went to college, I was there for three and a half years to get two and a half years of credit. I disliked taking courses that I had little or no interest in. I ran out of money, time, interest, and motivation. The subjects I needed to take no longer appealed to me. Then I found out that the University of Michigan had a real estate program comprised of sixteen courses. I enrolled, and for the first time in my life was studying something that I cared about and knew I had to learn, and it was easy for me to understand. At that time, in Detroit, the big employers were Ford, Chrysler, and General Motors; and they wouldn't even talk to you about employment unless you had a college degree.

The real estate course allowed me to learn exactly what I wanted and provided me with the self-motivation to excel. I had the intelligence and the desire to learn to organize and succeed in business more than simply be a production worker. I realized that I had an opportunity, and I didn't intend to let it pass by.

Positive Thinking and Motivation

Positive thinking goes hand in hand with motivation. When you approach challenges or tasks with a positive mindset, you are more likely to feel confident and capable of achieving your goals. A positive self-image and a record of accomplishment keep a "can-do" attitude alive. This thought process frequently builds your self-initiative and leads to a positive way of looking at all setbacks and challenges. You then have the motivation to turn adversity into advancement.

Every day, regardless of his or her job, everyone experiences setbacks or difficulties. It's often easy and convenient to blame others for your setbacks. When I was a Century 21 broker, interest rates increased to 18 percent; people were financially devastated.

Every one of my salesforce had enough fear, anxiety, and depression.. If I was down when I got to work or didn't have a happy smile, I was just part of the group. One day, one of my salespeople told me that she felt miserable and dejected by the current state of the market. I sat her down and said, "Look, we're having a challenging time. When you look at the production you've done, you're in the top 25 percent of the sales force. Don't quit. You'd be stepping out of a profession you belong in, and you're too much of a powerful person for that." When I was done, she opened her purse, took out her handkerchief, dried her eyes, and said, "Okay, I'll stay."

The fact that I could stay positive and keep my people motivated allowed us to stay in business when over 50 percent of real estate brokers in Michigan closed their doors. I said to my salespeople, "Think about that. None of us is so powerful that we can eliminate 50 percent of our competition in one year. The recession has done it for us. And if we survive, and we will, we will earn double the profit once people have the money and confidence to buy again." Sometimes, finding motivation is just a basic story that's so simple and clear that you can't miss it.

After those experiences, I learned that positivity often creates a positive environment and attracts positive people into your life. This helped reinforce my motivation and kept me on track to achieve my goals. When you surround yourself with positive people, they can provide you with support and encouragement, which can help to boost your confidence and motivation.

Discipline and Motivation

As discussed earlier in the book, strategic discipline also plays a key part in motivation. If you are realistic, have a disciplined mind, and cultivate written goals that you read daily, it is much easier to direct your positive thinking into motivation. The ability to believe in yourself and to review past accomplishments that you have achieved enhances your confidence to overcome obstacles.

Historical written references that you recorded are the tools that support your self-image as a mountain climber with a positive can-do attitude.

My colleague Cecilia and I have done this for years. Before we leave every day, we list ten good things that happened during the workday. We never count the bad things. Then, if we get depressed, we review our list of good things. I believe it keeps us going hour to hour because we're quickly reminded of our successes, giving us the power to continue.

Motivating Your Team

After you've found what motivates you, it is vital to focus on boosting your team. Your team is the heartbeat of an organization; and as mentioned in Chapter 2, leadership is significant to a company's success. I also want to stress the importance of keeping your team motivated. A motivated team will thrive.

*Take care of your troops,
and your troops will take care of you.*

When you praise and encourage others, you're building motivation. Some people work for money, freedom, and independence. Why make harmful habits? Why not create positive habits?

Motivation Vince-isms

- Provide feedback: Give constructive feedback to your team, both positive and negative. This can help them improve their skills and continue to be effective.

- Encourage self-care: Remind them to take care of themselves and prioritize self-care. This can include encouraging breaks, vacations, and stress-reducing activities.

- Provide growth opportunities: Offer opportunities for your team to learn new skills, take on new challenges, or lead new projects. This can keep them engaged and motivated in their role.

- Foster a positive work environment: Create a positive environment that supports their well-being and fosters community and collaboration. This can include team-building activities, open communication channels, and flexible work arrangements.

- Lead by example: As a leader, model the behavior and attitude that you want your team to emulate. Show enthusiasm and passion for the work, and demonstrate a commitment to the organization's mission and values. This can inspire the motivator to do the same.

CHAPTER 6

WIN-WIN

Key Principle: Responsible, good citizens usually enjoy better health and a happier, longer life because they resist resentment, retaliation, and reprisals, which are all negative in content and lead to negative thinking, negative action, and negative consequences.

"You can get anything you want in life if you help enough people get what they want."
—Zig Ziglar

When Walt Disney was alive, he was a master storyteller and a wizard with words. However, many people don't know how miserable his childhood was. Disney's father was negative and often overbearing. Because of this family situation, Disney promised himself that he'd do what he could to help others have a happier childhood than he had experienced. Disney is a fantastic example of the principle of "win-win." A win-win mentality is an approach to problem-solving and decision-making that seeks to find mutually beneficial outcomes for all parties involved. It involves recognizing and respecting the needs and interests of others and our own and finding creative solutions that address everyone's concerns. **The belief that there has to be a winner and a loser is one of the great misconceptions in the human mind**. If a deal, sale, or interaction is approached with sincerity and genuine interest in the other party, both parties can win. Countless personal development books express the idea that to receive, you must first give.

Abundance vs Scarcity Mindset

The first step to a win-win mentality is a shift in perspective from a scarcity mindset to one of abundance. The abundance and scarcity mindsets are two different ways of perceiving the world and your place in it.

An abundance mindset is characterized by the belief that there is enough of everything to go around. People with an abundance mindset tend to focus on opportunities and possibilities, believing their success and prosperity do not depend on others losing or failing. They are generally optimistic, grateful, and generous, and they view challenges as opportunities to learn and grow.

On the other hand, a scarcity mindset is characterized by the belief that resources are limited and that you must compete with others to get what you need. There were days when I was on such a strict budget that buying razor blades was a luxury. At some point, I read that steel corrodes when exposed to the weather. The article said that if you took your razor blades and soaked them in oil, they'd last almost forever. I had an old aspirin pill box that I put on my sink with some oil and a razor blade in there; and instead of getting three shaves per blade, I probably got close to a month's worth. Eventually I began to think about the opportunity cost of the whole endeavor. It took time to find the pillbox case, open it up, fill it with oil, fish the blades out, rinse them, and finally shave. What if, instead, I took that time to think about how effectively I could work to hire an extra salesperson, give them more training, be involved, and help them sell a buyer on signing the potential purchase agreement?

Rather than falling into a scarcity mindset and focusing on limitations and obstacles, I believed I could change my priorities and better succeed.

It's important to note that both mindsets are a matter of perspective and can be influenced by various factors such as upbringing, culture, experiences, and beliefs. Research suggests that individuals who adopt an abundance mindset are more likely to experience happiness, success, and well-being than those who adopt a scarcity mindset.

Now, this is probably not new information for many readers. Still, take a moment to reflect on your actions and choices over the last few months. Reevaluate your position, and don't just answer what you'd like to hear. Ask yourself: Do I exhibit a growth mindset or a fixed mindset?

The Law of Abundance

The law of abundance is simple: What you obtain or gather in the world is a small mathematical fraction of what exists. If you can double whatever your fraction is, your personal prosperity doubles. The amount of wealth, goodness, or choices in the world is endless. Maybe you can create something to share with more people using this principle.

We live on an earth of abundance. People say that people are starving because there's not enough food. That's not true. There's enough fruit falling from the trees to feed everybody in the world. There's not a shortage of food; there's a shortage of transportation, a shortage of government, fairness, taxation, and so on. **Friends help friends, and you have to be a friend to have a friend. If you help other people, they go out of their way to help you, your prosperity, and your confidence.** And as your money grows, you can spend less time worrying about what you don't have and more time trying to help others.

Seeking Wins

Growing up, my family didn't have the disposable income to buy candy bars. One day, a car accident happened on the street outside my house. My brother Robert and I ran to the window to see if the police would arrive at the scene, but instead, the doorbell rang, and lo and behold, the truck driver was standing there, holding a big box of Hershey Bars! The delivery driver explained that the bars were broken and couldn't be sold. When you're in the second grade and somebody gives you a giant Hershey bar, you don't care if it's broken. This man was the perfect example of someone seeking a win-win. He was under pressure and could've saved time by throwing the candy in the trash can at the end of the street. Instead, he had asked somebody on the road where a family with kids lived and decided to bring them to us. Most of the time, it only takes a couple of seconds to bring someone happiness. In a world where competition and conflict often leave us feeling isolated and disconnected, a win-win mentality offers a powerful antidote, reminding us of the power of cooperation and the beauty of shared success. Success is not a zero-sum game where one person's gain necessarily means another's loss.

Win-Win Vince-isms

- Identify the goals and priorities of all parties: The first step in creating a win-win situation is to identify the goals and priorities of all parties involved. This can include asking questions and listening to each party's words. Understanding what each party wants to achieve makes it easier to find a solution that satisfies everyone's priorities.

- Find common ground: Once the goals and priorities of all parties have been identified, the next step is to find common ground. This involves looking for areas where the interests of all parties overlap.

- Brainstorm solutions: After identifying common ground, the next step is to brainstorm potential solutions. This can involve generating a list of possible solutions and evaluating them based on how well they satisfy all parties' priorities. It's essential to remain open-minded during this process and to consider all options.

- Evaluate solutions: Once potential solutions have been identified, it's time to evaluate them. This involves looking at each solution's pros and cons and determining which best satisfies the priorities of all parties involved. It's important to consider all options carefully and to choose the solution that offers the most benefits to everyone.

- Negotiate and compromise: Finally, it's time to negotiate and compromise. This involves working together to find a solution that satisfies everyone's priorities. It may include some give-and-take, but the result should be a solution that benefits everyone.

CHAPTER 7

POSITIVITY

Key Principle: Your altitude is determined by your attitude.

*"Keep your face to the sunshine
and you cannot see a shadow"*
—Helen Keller

uppose there's half a glass of water sitting on the table in front of you. Is that glass half empty or half full? This question has been posed countless times, in countless ways, for good reason. As you probably know, viewing the glass as half empty may indicate a negative attitude, whereas viewing it as half full indicates a more positive approach. When you maintain a positive attitude, you tend to have a better outlook on life, which can help you cope better with stress, anxiety, and depression. People with positive attitudes also tend to be more pleasant to be around, which can lead to stronger and more fulfilling relationships with family, friends, and colleagues. Unfortunately, maintaining a positive attitude is often easier said than done. So, how do you maintain a positive outlook when things get difficult?

Attitude of Gratitude

One of the keys to cultivating positivity is to focus on gratitude. Gratitude involves recognizing the good in our lives and celebrating the little wins even in the midst of challenges or difficulties.

Intentionally practice an attitude of gratitude.

When we focus on what we are thankful for, we shift our attention away from negativity and toward positivity. About four years ago, I had a heart attack. After the fact, I talked to the doctor and asked, "What are some good things that I can find from this event?" My doctor said, "Well Vince, there are actually quite a few good things that happened. Number one, you did the right thing and called your primary care doctor." When I called my primary care doctor, she immediately asked me if I was able to drive. She instructed me to drive to the hospital, give the attendant my car, and go right to the emergency room. She sent all of my medical information to the doctors at Providence Hospital so that when I arrived, they took me right up to the operating room and determined what surgery I needed. In short, that primary care physician really helped save my life. After hearing all of this from my cardiologist, I chose to be grateful; I was actually *lucky* to have had a heart attack with access to some of the best medical care in the world. I'm an American citizen, English is my primary language, and the physician spoke the same language. Furthermore, the physician that happened to be on call had over twenty years' experience, taught medicine at Wayne State University, and had performed so many heart surgeries that he stopped keeping count. When you choose to implement a positive attitude of gratitude, a negative event like a heart attack can be reframed.

Another thing I like to remind myself is that I happened to be born at a time of high prosperity. Two hundred years ago, people didn't have computers, TVs, radios, cars, trains, airplanes, or indoor plumbing. Most of them lived and died within about two hundred miles of where they were born. When you think about it that way, how can you not be grateful and happy? You were born in a time where you can go to school for free in America. You were born in a society where there's enough food produced. I personally was born into a healthy and happy family.

When I was a kid, I had a family friend who was born blind. I once asked what it was like to be blind. Rather than focusing on the fact that he couldn't see, he said, "Vince, when you're blind, you develop other senses. My hearing is better than yours. I don't care if yours is very good; mine's better. I sometimes have a hard time earning a living, so I use the unique skills and adaptations I have to tune pianos. I can't drive, but there's public transportation and the buses make a special stop for me when the driver sees my white cane. Other people help me. Society helps me." This family friend was thankful for so much despite not being able to see. What about you? Do *you* take the time to appreciate the sight you have?

> *"The only thing worse than being blind is having sight but no vision."*
> —Helen Keller

If you stop to realize that you were born in America at a time of prosperity with enough food, clothing, medicine, education, and freedom, it's clear that there's so much to be grateful for.

Surround Yourself with Positivity

Another important factor in cultivating positivity in your day-to-day life is to surround yourself with positive people and experiences. One time, an employee came into my office and began to unload around ten minutes of complaints and negativity onto me. Like everyone, this person had their own set of problems: family problems, financial problems, education problems, discipline problems, health problems, who knows? It was clear that this employee just needed something and somebody to yell at. Afterwards, I said to my son Owen, "With that type of person, you just have to listen. Let it go through one ear out the other and think to yourself, that attitude isn't justified."

Attitudes are contagious. Is yours worth catching?

We all have bad days. An occasional complaint is fine, but if negativity continues, it's contagious and destructive.

It can spread. Suppose you have an employee you want to invest in who does good work but who has a tendency to be quite negative. Address the situation by imposing a time limit on complaints and negative thought processes. Encourage your team to keep an eye on how much time they spend being negative throughout the workday.

Why walk around with the turkeys when you can soar with the eagles?

To be successful, you need to surround yourself with positive, happy, productive people who are looking for solutions, not problems.

Everybody's looking for problems; they're easier to find than solutions. Psychiatrists say 80 percent of adult human beings in any country think negatively 80 percent of the time. Those who rise above the pack are people who try to turn that 80:20 ratio

---

"What you think about you bring about."

---

around. There's positive news everywhere. Just find it, read it, print it out, write it down, absorb it, and put it on a vision board.

Even in difficult times, it is possible to maintain a positive outlook by focusing on an attitude of gratitude and surrounding yourself with positive people. By cultivating positivity, you can tap into the power of your own mind to create a better, happier, and more fulfilling life.

Positivity Vince-isms

- Surround yourself with positivity: Spend time with people who uplift and inspire you. Seek out positive news and media and avoid negative influences as much as possible.

- Set positive goals: Setting goals that align with your values and that are attainable can give you a sense of purpose and motivation. Focus on what you want to achieve rather than what you fear.

- Reframe negative thoughts: Practice reframing negative thoughts into positive ones. Instead of focusing on what could go wrong, focus on what could go right. Challenge negative self-talk and replace it with positive affirmations.

- Engage in positive activities: Engage in activities that bring you joy and happiness, such as hobbies, spending time with loved ones, or volunteering. Doing things that make you feel good can help you stay positive and uplifted.

CHAPTER 8

RELATIONSHIPS

Key Principle: Rich relationships create a rich life.

"If you go looking for a friend, you're going to find they're scarce. If you go out to be a friend, you'll find them everywhere."
—Zig Ziglar

Hopefully, by this point in the book it's clear that my entire life has centered around relationships. I have striven my whole life to be a friend to all and continue to attempt to live in accordance with what Dale Carnegie teaches. My desk proudly sports a plaque that says, **"Never criticize, condemn, or complain."** My success has stemmed largely from the relationships I have formed, be they with teachers, peers, or leaders. As cheesy as it sounds, success is never achieved alone. Behind every great company there have been visionaries, operations individuals, administrators, sales reps, and efficiency experts. The ability to surround yourself with talented individuals is a true aspect of success, but just having talented people around isn't enough. ***Successful people surround themselves with talent and then keep that talent around.***

The only way to form lasting relationships is by genuinely wanting to help others win. As we mentioned earlier, people can spot in-

Are you someone with a life full of strong, powerful, fulfilling, and enjoyable relationships?

sincere appreciation; to be a friend you have to earn it, every day. I cannot stress enough the importance of forming *meaningful* relationships, not just *transactional*. The best way to make any relationship is to do something to help the other person. When someone has a positive experience with a person or a company, they are more likely to continue working with them in the future. This is because the person feels comfortable with the established relationship, and they are confident that the person or company will deliver on their promises. Doing business with someone you know, like, and trust can save time and effort and continue to build upon success. When you already have a connection with someone, you don't have to start from scratch getting to know them, their business style, and their values. People may also do business with people they know because they feel a sense of loyalty to them. This is particularly true in industries where relationships and personal connections play a significant role, such as in small businesses and family-run enterprises.

Helping the Inner Circle

It's always nice to help somebody solve their personal problems. It means even more if you help solve a problem for those close to them, such as their parents or children. When I was a real-estate agent, someone once called me up and said, "Hey Vince! I haven't talked to you in years, but my mom has a problem." Using my background and knowledge as a landlord, I was able to give them some compatible, reasonable solutions to the situation. If you do something to help someone's family, that person will never forget you. I've found that people usually want to return favors. Even though reciprocity isn't the reason you did them a favor in the first place, it can be a powerful shortcut to winning friends and influencing people.

Managing Others and Yourself

When you're eighteen, nineteen, twenty, or twenty-one, it's pretty difficult to manage anybody who's thirty or thirty-five. Oftentimes, they don't pay attention to you. I've found, though, that if I am sincere and honest with people, they pick up on it. It's then so easy for me to get them to feel that we are part of a team, part of a common effort, and that we combine our talents and share them. If I need to manage people older than I just come up and am totally open and honest when beginning the relationship.

When I was about twenty-three years old, I was doing appraisals for the FHA. I remember approaching my manager at the time, Jack Johnson, and saying, "Jack, do you live on the west side of Detroit?" He said, "No, I live on the north side. I've worked on the west side for years now." Now, I was open and honest. I said, "I'm on the west side of Detroit trying to compare subdivisions. Jack, you have more experience in that neighborhood than I do. Which one of the subdivisions would you say, based on your knowledge and experience, is more valuable today?" He helped me right away. I like to think that he recognized that I was open, fair, honest, and trying to be a team player. That was a positive turning point in our relationship. He helped me because I recognized and stated that he had more knowledge on the topic than I did.

A little while later, I was trying to grow in the job. Unfortunately, the manager of the foreclosure department wouldn't assign me more responsibility until I had been there at least three years. I eventually got so frustrated that I went to my supervisor, Jack Johnson, and said, "Can you talk to these people in the foreclosure department and tell them I am competent enough to do more complex work?" Jack got up from his desk and talked to the man in charge. He promised, "If you give Vince the opportunity to learn more difficult cases, I'll personally help him myself. If he doesn't qualify, we'll take him off the assignment."

Somehow, I had established goodwill with my boss just by doing, learning, and studying what I was supposed to. Our relationship had been so strengthened that he went out of his way to place me in another department where I could learn more and expand my opportunities.

The bottom line is that entering a relationship in openness, honesty, and hard work will have exponential returns. Rather than trying to be the smartest in the room or taking shortcuts, ask questions and learn from those who've gone before you.

Ending a Relationship

Unfortunately, not all relationships are positive. I'm sure everyone has had that one friend, colleague, or employee who requires more energy than they give back. As I mentioned in the chapter on positivity, negative thoughts and actions can spread, whether it's to your team or your subconscious, so ending relationships the right way is an extremely useful skill to have. When I realize that I am being used, either in a friendship or by a so-called "professional networker," the most important thing is to remain polite. While I don't want to continue the relationship, I also don't want to alienate or hurt anyone's feelings. My usual response goes something like this: "Respectfully, my time is valuable and so is yours. I believe we are both better off dropping this conversation and seeking cooperation from different sources. I wish you the best of luck and success in the future." Remaining calm and polite allows everyone to win, even though the relationship is not continuing. My approach to firing is a little bit different, but the underlying principles remain the same. Whenever I have to fire people, I first analyze the situation from a place of empathy and compassion. I then make a conscious effort to frame the situation in a positive light.

I often say something like this: "Today's actually a good day for you and me. It's obvious through your actions that you're not happy here. That's okay, though, because you have greatness in you, and now you're free to go be great in another endeavor. I don't want to be the guy who held you up from living the life of your dreams. Since you're obviously not happy here, and we're not happy with your performance, it's time for us to part ways, effective immediately. I'll always support you because I believe you have greatness in you." Using this method, people, when I have fired them, are often hugging and crying with me. To me, the most important thing is helping others get ahead in life. This doesn't mean that you have to continue relationships that are negatively impacting you or your business, it means that you should approach every relationship with the other person in mind. Whether it be beginning a new relationship or ending an old one, strive to be open, honest, and positive.

Relationship Vince-isms:

- Help someone when it is needed, not just when it is convenient.

- Express your willingness to further assist if requested.

- Be sincere. A true friend will help you even if it is not in their own best interest.

- When people observe you having a "what-can-I-do-to-help-you-in-need" philosophy and have it as part of your personality, they embrace wanting to know and communicate and associate with you, and it raises their cooperative spirit and their willingness to sacrifice for you because you will sacrifice for them.

CHAPTER 9

KNOWLEDGE

Key Principle: Education comes in many forms and knowledge is all around you. There is no "right" way to learn.

"Knowledge is not power…unless it is put to use"
—Napoleon Hill

I f we never received any fresh, new ideas from others, our only options would be to keep doing things the same way we've always done them. It's quite simple—the key to success is new information. New information stimulates both our reasoning processes and our creative juices and helps us think better. We can get information from our own experiences or from other people, either in the form of advice or books.

Learning from Books
As I realized after reading *How to Win Friends and Influence People* by Dale Carnegie, a lot of the time, the struggles that we go through are not unique. Other individuals have experienced them before. **Through reading books you can learn through the experiences of others. If you can read the stories of someone else who's been through a similar struggle, it's a shortcut. The great thing here is that the advice from these resources is immortalized in print and available at little to no cost.** Please see the appendix for a list of my ten

You can learn from advice or you can learn from experience, but experience is a much harder teacher.

favorite and most impactful books. Experience is a much harder teacher. If reading isn't your thing, approaching others for their experience is just as beneficial; find a mentor, hire a coach, or join a mastermind alliance.

Learning from Others

As the earlier chapters have established, I was never a very good student. Sure, my strengths lie elsewhere, but I have definitely had my fair share of learning from my experiences the hard way. School teaches you basic subjects: math, chemistry, biology, and literature, etc. Those never interested me; I always wanted to learn about business, how to more effectively work with people, and how to help myself and others be more successful.

"If you are not willing to learn, no one can help you. If you are determined to learn, no one can stop you."
—Zig Ziglar

I began to realize that people with more academic knowledge and skill, who seemed to be quicker readers, better spellers, and writers, couldn't rally people as quickly as I could. I could sell ideas; I was the president of a high school youth club, and I probably was the least adept at getting brochures out to promote a dance, hire a band, and reserve the hall. But it was easy for me to go up to different people and say, "Hey Charlie or Betty, you're good at this stuff and I need your expertise. It's probably a lot of work and no compensation, but you're contributing toward the growth and stability of this group. Could you possibly help me with this or get a volunteer to take over this aspect of the project?" This action was easy for me to accomplish. So, as mentioned in the previous section, I recognized the power of reading. I began strategically selecting books from some of the great leaders, motivators, and entrepreneurs of the time. I read their books; learned their principles; and, more importantly, put them into practice. Knowledge is nothing if it's not used.

Many people go through life without thinking twice about what they don't know. I naturally had curiosity in abundance throughout my life. It is that curiosity that leads you to the right questions and ultimately the right answers. However, when you get a bit older and study different things, whether you like them or not, you come to the conclusion that even the smartest person in the world only knows a little of their own subjects. Take me for example. I know quite a bit about real estate and mortgages. I know nothing about welding or repairs, electrical currents, or weather patterns. People's knowledge can be deep but limited in scope. So, I quickly came to the conclusion that if I have the ability to get along with people, **all I have to do is find somebody who's an expert on the topic I want to learn about. If I share information that I have and make a friend, they'll reciprocate.** It is just amazing to me how many people have so many talents that I obviously don't have. Just as amazing is how willing they are to cooperate in your promotion as long as you appreciate, recognize, and acknowledge what they do. Sometimes I look around a business and I see all the different jobs in the different categories and different specialties and say I don't qualify for a job in any one of these departments; but I work effectively with the people who can get the work done. Learning from others and making connections is one of the easiest ways to get assistance without having to become an expert yourself. **I take advice from anybody who I believe has more knowledge than I do on the topic**. I don't care about their religion, nationality, age, color, or sex. If somebody has more knowledge than I, and they're willing to share it, I appreciate their sharing it and I always want to give them recognition and express my gratitude for their sharing their knowledge with me.

"If you have knowledge, let others light their candles in it." —Margaret Fuller

---

Once, I was in Italy with my daughter. Her children went to a school run by the Italian government. Half the class was in Italian and half of it was in English. One day at the dinner table, my youngest grandson, Benjamin, was correcting his older brother in Italian pronunciation and grammar. His older brother got mad and said, "Mom, why do I have to listen to him? He's only a first grader." My daughter handled it perfectly. She said, "Evan, you might as well learn this when you're young." Anytime anybody has knowledge, and they're trying to correct you in a professional manner to assist you, it's nice to say thank you. It doesn't matter if they're younger or older or of a different religion, nationality, or occupation. If they're willing to help advance you, you can at least recognize it. In the words of seventeenth-century poet John Donne, "No man is an island." Most highly successful people will tell you that they could not have even begun their journey without the encouragement, support, and advice of the people around them. Admit what you don't know, ask for advice, and appreciate experience. When you come to somebody humbly seeking their advice and experience, they're more likely to share with you. You're simply appreciating everything they've gone through to get to that point. Be nice to people, have a lot of friends, and be willing to share knowledge with others.

Learning from Coaches

Another way to benefit from the experience of others is through paid advisors or coaches. Jim Rohn once said, "**It's not as bad to not read a book in the last ninety days as it is to not read a book in the last ninety days and think it doesn't matter**." **You can apply the same logic to coaching: "It's not as bad to not have a coach as it is to not have a coach and think it doesn't matter."** As a coach, I've personally benefited from Tony Jeary, Carl White, and Dale Vermillion. So, while I've had a mentor and a coach and believe in the usefulness of both, I want to stress the importance in fully vetting that individual. You need to be sure the mentor or coach is truly an expert in their field and truly has the knowledge you need and the willingness to share it.

Sharing Knowledge

Later in life, once I became successful and had my own business, I put a table by the door stacked with my favorite and most impactful books. Whenever anyone comes to see me, I offer them a book and ask that when they read it, they give me a call and discuss it with me. I *believe there's no point in holding knowledge; one of my goals is to make as many millionaires as possible in my life by sharing what I know, hence the title of this book.*

The thing about knowledge is the necessity of separating basic knowledge, like laws of mathematics, from nonspecific knowledge, like knowledge of human nature and how people are going to react if they're treated in a certain way. Knowledge is changing so rapidly. People say knowledge is power, but the really tuned-in people know that knowledge is potential power. Knowledge is not power unless you use it the correct way. Nobody has a monopoly on knowledge.

In short, good advice is often the best teacher. **The wise person strategically listens to those who are willing to share their experiences, expertise, and recommendations to help him or her win**. The benefit of gaining wisdom and knowledge from someone else's years of experience can make an amazing difference in your journey toward happiness and millionaire status.

Knowledge Vince-isms

- Read regularly: Reading books, articles, and other written material on a regular basis is one of the best ways to gain knowledge. Make a habit of setting aside time each day to read something new.

- Attend classes or workshops: Attending classes or workshops in a particular field can provide you with hands-on learning opportunities and access to experts in the field. Look for courses or workshops in your community or online.

- Take courses on whatever platform you are most comfortable with: Many universities and online learning platforms offer free or low-cost courses on a wide range of topics. These courses can be a great way to gain knowledge in a structured and self-paced format.

- Listen to podcasts: Podcasts are a great way to learn about a wide range of topics from history to science to personal development. Look for podcasts that are relevant to your interests and listen to them regularly.

- Ask questions: Don't be afraid to ask questions of experts or individuals who have knowledge in a particular area. Ask for advice, feedback, or resources to help you gain more knowledge.

- Practice active listening: Listening actively to others can help you gain knowledge and understanding of different perspectives and ideas. Make a conscious effort to listen actively and seek to understand others' viewpoints.

CHAPTER 10
SMILE

Key Principle: A smile conveys friendship, acceptance, open-mindedness, and the fact that you are in a good mood.

"Smile at everyone you meet."
—Mother Teresa

Have you ever noticed how a simple smile can change the mood of a room or improve your day? Smiling is a powerful tool that can positively impact our personal and professional relationships. We smile when we feel happy, and we smile when we want to make others feel happy.

I was about five years old when I realized the power of a smile. And I've frankly used it all my life. I think it's part of my personality. I also think it saves a lot of time because it conveys everything that I intend to discuss with someone. Humans are programmed to smile and respond to smiles. When people have a newborn, they always say, "Smile!" As human beings, we learn to smile within two or three weeks, certainly years before we learn to speak. So, the power of the smile, from a baby to an adult, is universal and powerful—it's the first form of communication we learn. I remember that in college we were learning about the Dewey Decimal System and the quickest way to find the right book in the library. I was bored to death.

I couldn't tune in or pay attention. Suddenly, the instructor said, "This is part of your homework assignment. Go to the library and find the book that I assigned to you. The librarian has to check what time you came into the library and how long it took you to get the book." I immediately thought, "Oh no! I should've paid attention in class," but I went to the library. Eventually, the librarian walks over to me. Instinctively I smiled, and she smiled back and asked, "What's on your mind?" I said, "Well, I came over here with an assignment, but I just have to be honest and tell you I never knew how difficult your job was." Next I said, "I also thought, what lovely red hair you have. My aunt has hair just like it!" I thought I was making progress. Smiling, the librarian asked, "What's your problem?"

I explained my homework assignment, and she looked at her watch and then led me to the right aisle, cabinet, and shelf. She handed me the book and wrote down a time of one and a half minutes. When I went to class, it was one of the few times I did better than all the other students. The average time was about five to six minutes! After those experiences, I knew there was power in a smile.

Another secret of smiling is that it can give you a head start in human communications. Smiles are instantly conveyed; and regardless of what nationality you are, what language you speak, what income range you're in, or what your occupation is, it's a universal language.

My wife and I took a trip to Europe. English is our primary language, but my wife, Chris, speaks a little Polish. We did okay in Poland but noticed that other European countries had little pa-

"Be helpful when you see a person without a smile, give them yours."
—Zig Ziglar

tience for those who don't speak their language. I'm not good at languages, so I smiled, and they had much more patience with me. Another time, my wife and I were totally lost in Italy. We were going the wrong way down one street, and the car that approached us was a police car. When they pulled me over I got out, shrugged my shoulders, gave them my driver's license, and smiled. They tried to speak with me in Italian and realized I couldn't understand them. So, they got someone else in the department on the police radio, and she communicated with us in English. And the police were so kind; we didn't get a ticket. They escorted us around a bridge off the one-way street onto the highway we were supposed to be on and pointed the way we were supposed to go! That's how I realized smiling can get you out of a tough situation. A smile is the first thing you notice. Whomever you're speaking to knows that you're open-minded and in a good mood, which usually puts them in a good mood. It puts you on a standard wavelength. When people transact, do business, communicate, and spend social time with people they feel comfortable with, a smile sends the message, "I'm not your enemy. I have nothing to hide. We're friends, we're

acquaintances." I have "SMILE" on my office wall for this very reason!

I also don't recall anybody ever signing a paper to buy a house or get a mortgage when the sales associate is unhappy. Anytime you're making a sales presentation of a product or service, try a smile before a handshake. Some people don't like to shake hands, but when you smile, sometimes they put out their hand, signaling that they want to express a happy mood.

Smiles are much more than just a facial expression. They have the power to communicate emotions, build relationships, and even improve our physical and mental health. Smiling releases endorphins, the feel-good hormones that promote a sense of happiness and relaxation. Even when we don't feel happy, simply putting on a smile can help us feel better. Studies have also shown that smiling can have a positive impact on our personal and professional success. A study conducted by Hewlett Packard found that employees who smiled frequently were perceived as more confident and competent and were more likely to be promoted. From a simple gesture of kindness to a genuine expression of happiness, a smile can have a profound impact on ourselves and those around us. By understanding the science and psychology behind smiling, we can harness the power of this universal language to create more positive interactions and enhance our overall well-being. So remember to smile often, even in the face of adversity, as it is a small act that can make a big difference in your life and in the lives of those you encounter. Whether at work, with friends and family, or interacting with strangers, a smile is a powerful tool that can help you live a happier, healthier, and more fulfilling life.

SMILE Vince-Isms

- Think positive thoughts: Positive thoughts and emotions can help bring a smile to your face naturally. Try to focus on positive things in your life, and practice and express gratitude regularly.

- Surround yourself with positive people: Being around positive and uplifting people can help put you in a good mood and make it easier to smile. Seek out people who make you feel good about yourself and who bring joy to your life.

- Find humor in everyday situations: Humor can be a great way to bring a smile to your face. Look for opportunities to find humor in everyday situations, and don't take yourself too seriously.

- Be kind to yourself and others: Being kind to yourself and others can help foster positive emotions and make it easier to smile. Look for opportunities to be kind to others, and practice self-compassion when things don't go as planned."

Conclusion

Writing this book has been a lifelong dream of mine. I've always wanted to write a book about life experiences and somehow tie it in with business opportunities, but like 99 percent of adults who have that desire, I've never seemed to be able to start and complete the project. With Tony Jeary's encouragement and assistance, Cecilia Morelli's intuitive insights, and the cooperative skills of Ella and Daniel, I've been able to fulfill that goal and share my journey with you. For me, and probably for you, my home is my sanctuary. The real estate industry has given me the incredible opportunity to create generational wealth, build a legacy, and help my family. I want the same for you. I have spent countless decades reading, learning, and living personal development. I've had massive successes and catastrophic failures yet have learned all the while. My hope is this book has served as a guide to my beliefs and mindset. Above all else remember, as Zig Ziglar said, "You can get anything in the world you want if you help enough people get what they want."

Allow your dreams to unfold as life moves forward in pursuit of a bigger vision, but never lose sight of those around you. Approach life with an "others first" mindset and reap the rewards that come from openness, honesty, and sincerity. Adversities will keep happening in life; and while you continue to build your business and legacy, fall in love with life's journey and have a willingness to evolve as time progresses. Behind every ending lies the start of a new relationship and opportunity.

One final note: In my opinion, sometimes it is better to share goals, BUT some goals maybe should be kept private. Examples would be family goals, etc.

THREE OF MY GOALS THAT I WOULD LIKE TO LEAVE YOU WITH:

1. Long life. Happy Death. Favorable Judgement.

2. I aspire to inspire before I expire.

3. To be a teenager again. Since I cannot go backward, I have to go forward and live to be at least 113 to reach this goal.

We can help each other reach each other's goals. By expressing these thoughts it will help us both live longer.

Send me an email at vince@smprate.com. I am interested in you and your goals and what I can do to help you.

Acknowledgments

There are so many people who go into the creation of a book. I appreciate all of those who've contributed. I'd especially like to thank my wife, Christine, for all of the times she allowed me to express my views on this topic. Writing a book often takes away from family time, and I greatly appreciate Christine's patient input and commentary. I'd also like to acknowledge my daughter, Bridget Stockton, and my son, Owen Lee, for their continued support of my wife and me in our life activities and their efforts to make the world a better place.

My daughter Bridget and her husband Don are successfully raising three boys, Evan, Benjamin, and Vincent, all of whome have enjoyed success in life, whether in education or the business world. Owen and his wife, Heather, have raised a successful daughter, Maura, and two successful sons, Patrick and Declan. They have all accelerated and achieved success in their respective fields of endeavor. My six grandchildren are all good citizens and share different successes in different degrees in academics, athletics, music, and the arts.

Additionally, Cecilia Morelli has been a strong and invaluable contributor to the factual information and life experiences that I've expressed in this book. Finally, without the expertise of wordsmiths like Tony Jeary, Daniel Marold, and Ella Imrie, this book could never have been written.

I believe everybody has a book in them! I am looking forward to reading yours!

Enthusiastically,
VINCE

Appendix

The following resources are hand-picked by me to help you, the future millionaire. I hope they compound upon the lessons taught in this book and bring you closer to success.

Key Principles

1. Today's dream could be tomorrow's achievement. Nothing is accomplished without belief.

2. Leaders must believe, persuade, and have discipline and persistence.

3. All three (know, like, and trust) must be present in a successful sale; two won't work.

4. Survive, then thrive.

5. A clear goal with a realistic timetable is the tool that defeats inertia and overcomes obstacles.

6. Responsible, good citizens usually enjoy better health and a happier, longer life because they resist resentment, retaliation, and reprisals, which are all negative in content and lead to negative thinking, negative action, and negative consequences.

7. Your altitude is determined by your attitude.

8. Rich relationships create a rich life.

9. Education comes in many forms and knowledge is all around you. There is no "right" way to learn.

10. A smile conveys friendship, acceptance, open-mindedness, and the fact that you are in a good mood.

Vince-Ism Compilation

Mindset Vince-isms

- Embrace a growth mindset: Adopting a growth mindset means seeing failures and setbacks as opportunities to learn and grow. You believe that your skills and abilities can be developed through dedication and hard work rather than just innate talent.

- Take action: Success doesn't come from just thinking about it; it comes from taking action. Create a plan, set achievable goals, and take consistent steps towards them.

- Learn from failure: Instead of dwelling on failures and setbacks, use them as opportunities to learn and grow. Analyze what went wrong, identify the lessons learned, and use that knowledge to do better next time.

- Stay persistent: Success takes time and effort. Stay persistent and keep working toward your goals, even when it's tough. Remember that setbacks and failures are a natural part of the journey, and keep pushing forward.

Leadership Vince-isms

- Communication: A great leader is an excellent communicator. Communication is key to effectively delegating tasks, providing feedback, and inspiring a team to work toward a common goal. Effective communication also involves being an active listener and understanding the needs and concerns of team members.

- Lead by example: Great leaders lead by example. They set the standard for their team by demonstrating a strong work ethic, a positive attitude, and a commitment to achieving goals. When leaders model the behavior they expect from their team, it inspires them to do the same.

- Develop your team: Great leaders focus on developing their team members. They invest time and resources into their professional growth and provide opportunities for them to learn new skills and take on new challenges. Leaders who prioritize the development of their team build a more skilled and motivated workforce.

- Build trust: Trust is an essential component of effective leadership. Leaders who build trust with their team members create a positive and productive work environment. Trust is built through consistent actions, transparency, and honest communication.

- Empower your team: Empowering team members means giving them the autonomy to make decisions and take ownership of their work. When team members feel empowered, they are more motivated and invested in their work.

Know, Like, and Trust Vince-isms

- Be humble: Humility is an important quality to have when sharing your knowledge with others. Acknowledge that you don't know everything and be open to learning from others.

- Share your knowledge selectively: Be mindful of the appropriate time and place to share your knowledge. Only interject during conversations if you have something valuable to contribute.

- Listen actively: Be an active listener when others are speaking. Show interest in what they have to say and ask thoughtful questions. This helps build rapport and establish mutual respect.

- Be respectful: Respect others' opinions and perspectives even if you disagree with them. Avoid belittling or dismissing others' ideas, which can be arrogant and disrespectful.

- Stay curious: Keep an open mind about the world around you. This can help you to continue learning and growing while also staying humble.

- Provide social proof: Share testimonials from people who have consumed your products or services. Share stories of how you successfully helped others achieve results.

- Be transparent: Let people see who and what you are—and who and what you're not.

- Be accessible: Place your contact details on every conspicuous possible place you can.

Resiliency Vince-isms

- Build a support team: Having a strong support network of family, friends, or colleagues can help you through difficult times. Reach out to trusted individuals when you need support or advice.

- Focus on the present: It's easy to get caught up in worrying about the future or ruminating on past mistakes. However, focusing on the present moment can help you build resiliency by reducing stress and anxiety.

- Practice gratitude: Cultivating a sense of gratitude can help shift your focus from negative to positive. Taking time to appreciate the good things in your life can help you maintain a positive outlook even during challenging times.

- Learn from setbacks: Resilient individuals view setbacks and failures as opportunities for growth and learning. Reflecting on what went wrong and what you can do differently next time can help you build resiliency and improve your chances of success in the future.

- Stay optimistic: Maintaining a positive outlook can help you build resiliency by keeping you motivated and hopeful even in the face of adversity. Instead of focusing on what could go wrong, focus on the opportunities and possibilities that exist.

Motivation Vince-isms

- Provide feedback: Give constructive feedback to your team, both positive and negative. This can help them improve their skills and continue to be effective.

- Encourage self-care: Remind them to take care of themselves and prioritize self-care. This can include encouraging breaks, vacations, and stress-reducing activities.

- Provide growth opportunities: Offer opportunities for your team to learn new skills, take on new challenges, or lead new projects. This can keep them engaged and motivated in their role.

- Foster a positive work environment: Create a positive environment that supports their well-being and fosters community and collaboration. This can include team-building activities, open communication channels, and flexible work arrangements.

- Lead by example: As a leader, model the behavior and attitude you want your team to emulate. Show enthusiasm and passion for the work, and demonstrate a commitment to the organization's mission and values. This can inspire the motivator to do the same.

Win-Win Vince-isms

- Identify the goals and priorities of all parties: The first step in creating a win-win situation is to identify the goals and priorities of all parties involved. This can include asking questions and listening to each party's words. Understanding what each party wants to achieve makes it easier to find a solution that satisfies everyone's priorities.

- Find common ground: Once the goals and priorities of all parties have been identified, the next step is to find common ground. This involves looking for areas where the interests of all parties overlap.

- Brainstorm solutions: After identifying common ground, the next step is to brainstorm potential solutions. This can involve generating a list of possible solutions and evaluating them based on how well they satisfy all parties' priorities. It's essential to remain open-minded during this process and to consider all options.

- Evaluate solutions: Once potential solutions have been identified, it's time to evaluate them. This involves looking at each solution's pros and cons and determining which best satisfies the priorities of all parties involved. It's important to consider all options carefully and to choose the solution that offers the most benefits to everyone.

- Negotiate and compromise: Finally, it's time to negotiate and compromise. This involves working together to find a solution that satisfies everyone's priorities. It may include some give-and-take, but the result should be a solution that benefits everyone.

Positivity Vince-isms

- Surround yourself with positivity: Spend time with people who uplift and inspire you. Seek out positive news and media and avoid negative influences as much as possible.

- Set positive goals: Setting goals that align with your values and that are attainable can give you a sense of purpose and motivation. Focus on what you want to achieve rather than what you fear.

- Reframe negative thoughts: Practice reframing negative thoughts into positive ones. Instead of focusing on what could go wrong, focus on what could go right. Challenge negative self-talk and replace it with positive affirmations.

- Engage in positive activities: Engage in activities that bring you joy and happiness, such as hobbies, spending time with loved ones, or volunteering. Doing things that make you feel good can help you stay positive and uplifted.

Relationship Vince-isms

- Help someone when it is needed, not just when it is convenient.

- Express your willingness to further assist if requested.

- Be sincere. A true friend will help you even if it is not in their own best interest.

- When people observe you having a "what-can-I-do-to-help-you-in-need" philosophy, and you have it as part of your personality, they embrace wanting to know and communicate and associate with you; and it raises their cooperative spirit and their willingness to sacrifice for you because you will sacrifice for them.

Knowledge Vince-isms

- Read regularly: Reading books, articles, and other written material on a regular basis is one of the best ways to gain knowledge. Make a habit of setting aside time each day to read something new.

- Attend classes or workshops: Attending classes or workshops in a particular field can provide you with hands-on learning opportunities and access to experts in various fields. Look for courses or workshops in your community or online.

- Take online courses: Many universities and online learning platforms offer free or low-cost courses on a wide range of topics. These courses can be a great way to gain knowledge in a structured and self-paced format.

- Listen to podcasts: Podcasts are a great way to learn about a wide range of topics, from history to investing to personal development, etc. Look for podcasts that are relevant to your interests and listen to them regularly.

- Ask questions: Don't be afraid to ask questions of experts or individuals who have knowledge in a particular area. Ask for advice, feedback, or resources to help you gain more knowledge.

- Practice active listening: Listening actively to others can help you gain knowledge and understanding of different perspectives and ideas. Make a conscious effort to listen actively and seek to understand others' viewpoints.

SMILE Vince-Isms

- Think positive thoughts: Positive thoughts and emotions can help bring a smile to your face naturally. Try to focus on positive things in your life, and practice an attitude of gratitude.

- Surround yourself with positive people: Being around positive and uplifting people can help put you in a good mood and make it easier to smile. Seek out people who make you feel good about yourself and who bring joy to your life.

- Find humor in everyday situations: Humor can be a great way to bring a smile to your face. Look for opportunities to find humor in everyday situations, and don't take yourself too seriously.

- Be kind to yourself and others: Being kind to yourself and others can help foster positive emotions and make it easier to smile. Look for opportunities to be kind to others, and practice self-compassion when things don't go as planned.

Strategic Business Cards

Business cards, if used strategically, can be a useful tool for networking and establishing connections in a professional setting.

Personally, I have two business cards. When I first meet people, I try to create a humorous image and get them to laugh and look at my picture, since a picture's worth a thousand words. I often tell them two "boring" things. First, I finished high school; and second, I'm not cheap, but I'm frugal. This doesn't usually impress anybody. To prove my point, I show them my business card with my high school picture on it. I explain, "When I was in high school, we had a good photog-

rapher, and he took a complimentary picture. That's why I use this on my business card." People usually look at it and laugh.

And I say, "That's the good news. And the bad news is, a couple of years ago I was informed by the state of Michigan that that picture is borderline fraud. They asked me to get a new picture." And then I hand them my second business card and mention, "This one just shows that I respect the law!"

And then they never forget you.

Vince's Most Influential Quotes and Sayings

Quotes

I believe in you. I believe in me. I believe in SMP. —Vince Lee

If it goes unstated, it goes unnoticed. —Darryl Turner

Luck is the residue of design and desire. —John Milton

Smile. It benefits both the sender and the receiver, and it costs nothing. —Vince Lee

Be prepared. —Lord Robert Baden-Powell (Boy Scout oath)

Learn from the past, live in the present, and plan for the future. —Zig Ziglar

If a picture is worth a thousand words, a visit is worth a thousand pictures. —Vince Lee

You can have everything in life you want if you will just help enough other people get what they want first. —Zig Ziglar

Sayings

The most important piece of information on a document is the date. (The reason for this is that time and circumstances change, and it represents a picture of events that were in place as of that date.)

Ninety percent of all human knowledge is absorbed through the eyes. (Remember: when you are selling, use charts and graphs. When you tell stories, people will get impressions of your presentation because they visualize in word pictures.)

10 Recommended Books for the Future Millionaires and High Achievers

1. *How to Win Friends and Influence people—Dale Carnegie*

- I was not getting along well with my father at this time because I thought my father, with his ability to charm, intelligence, and creativity, spent too much time in a negative thought process.

- My dad kept thinking that my being friendly and supportive of people and their ideas was just an easier way to make friends and to get assistance and support from other people.

- When I was sixteen years old, a junior in high school, I read the book and was totally amazed that someone who had similar viewpoints as mine had developed his thoughts into a whole philosophy of action. His words helped thousands of people overcome all sorts of adversity. His ideas developed harmony, tranquility, and happiness while dealing with everyday work and life struggles.

2. *How to Stop Worrying and Start Living—Dale Carnegie*

- I found out that the chapter dealing with how to stop worrying and start living was one chapter in his initial book, and this one chapter appealed to more people than any other chapter for two reasons:

  ☐ It dealt with how to overcome the problems of worry.

  ☐ It was the biggest problem that most readers of the book encountered, a consistent habit of negative worry. I read and reread the chapter, and fortunately for me, I was at a formative stage of life; thus, his thoughts helped me create habits of positive thinking and goal setting.

3. The Magic of Believing—Claude Bristol

- Claude Bristol introduced me to a new psychological depth of thought in relationship to the power of the subconscious mind and to the realization that forces existed that, through the power of imagination, could bring into existence positive situations and successes that initially seemed beyond the realm of reason.

4. The Strangest Secret—Earl Nightingale

- Earl Nightingale had a tougher childhood than I did. Apparently, his father deserted his mother and him at a young age. To help relieve his mother's economic burden supporting him, he lied about his age and joined the army at seventeen.

- All of a sudden, he had clean clothing, a permanent place to sleep, three meals a day, and secure employment in the US Army; and he was fortunate enough to be stationed in the most beautiful place that he ever visited—Hawaii.

- Life changes drastically. Part of his assignment was to work on the battleship Arizona; and one beautiful Sunday morning, December 7, 1941, they were attacked by the Japanese Navy and Air Force in Pearl Harbor.

- His life instantly changed—There were 2,115 US military men who died on the ship that day, and he was one of only 112 who survived.

- He questioned why he lived when such a high percentage of fellow servicemen died. In his mind, there had to be a reason why he lived, so he searched for the reason.

- He searched for the secret as to why he was alive while others died. He came to the conclusion that he needed to make a contribution in life. He researched throughout history and came to the conclusion that "Anyone can alter their position in life by altering their state of mind." The secret, to him, was that an individual had control of his or her destiny. The more he studied ancient philosophers, he realized that his secret was really not a secret at all, and that this idea had been taught by philosophers and academics in different countries throughout the world for centuries.

5. *The Power of Positive Thinking—Norman Vincent Peale*

- This book was published in 1952, when I was in high school.

- I remember the author was being introduced on a Sunday morning TV show. I was excited about his presentation because his explanation of the content of the book seemed clear and convincing to me. I remember being surprised at the amount of criticism that he received. He was criticized for giving people false hopes. Reverend Peale was patient, diplomatic, and persuasive in addressing the attackers of his philosophy. This only convinced me more of the truth and power of his words.

- He is perhaps one of the best and most widely recognized motivational speakers of the twentieth century.

6. *Thank God Ahead of Time—Michael Crosby*

- Father Solanus was born in 1870 and died in Detroit in 1957.

- He was the sixth of sixteen born in an Irish immigrant family. Six girls and ten boys.

- He always wanted to be a Catholic priest, but in the novitiates, he was never an excellent student. He could barely pass his exams. Ultimately, his superiors decided that he could become a priest but only with limited responsibilities; for instance, he couldn't preach or teach church doctrine.

- The turning point in the story is that his superiors tried to find a job that he could do and that he was qualified for with his limited education and abilities. The only job they could find for him was that of a porter of St. Bonaventure Church.

Father Solanus would answer the door and keep appointments for other priests and other similar jobs.

■ The provincial minister at St. Bonaventure's Parish in Detroit was the spiritual head of the Capuchin order in Michigan. One day, he realized that more people were coming to St. Bonaventure to see Fr. Solanus than to see him.

■ Father Solanus had minimum responsibilities; he mostly just heard confessions. He basically helped working families, mostly auto factory employees, in Detroit and Windsor, Canada. When he died, the Detroit police were called out to help the funeral director handle the crowds. Visiting hours were extended, and funeral services to handle the crowds were increased to three days. The Detroit Police estimated that approximately 6,000 working Detroiters came to his funeral. He truly helped thousands of people on a one-to-one basis. He helped organize and start the Capuchin soup kitchen at St. Bonaventure for free meals to feed the thousands of unemployed people during the depression years of the 1930s.

It wasn't the rich, it wasn't the politically connected, it was just the average auto worker with their day-to-day problems with family, budget, or health that he helped. Many favors or miracles were attributed to Fr. Solanus's intervention.

If you truly believe in miracles, take the time to read the book. Imagine one person in one lifetime aiding thousands of people to the degree that approximately 6,000 people took time out of their daily lives to attend his funeral.

7. *Tough Times Never Last, but Tough People Do—Rev. Schuller*

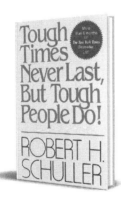

■ Rev. Schuller gave a talk to a group of farmers, some of whom were behind on their taxes on their farmland and were in jeopardy of losing their farms, which had been in their family for years. Rev. Schuller was requested by a local minister to rekindle faith and give some optimism and hope to depressed farmers. He had prepared a good sermon for the occasion, but when he got up to give it, he realized he left the notes in his other suit, so he had to give an impromptu talk. He said that when he was done with the talk, everyone left the church, and he didn't know if his talk was helpful to the parishioners. When he went outside of the church, he was surprised to see hundreds of parishioners who were waiting to congratulate him and thank him for bringing renewed hope to their depressed state.

Rev. Schuller said that when he and his wife were journeying home, his wife said that if the talk was so well received, they could help a lot of other people with the same talk by just putting it in a book. If they could get the book published, maybe it could bring help to thousands in different situations of despair. When Rev. Schuller asked his wife about what title she would suggest, she suggested, "Tough Times Never Last, but Tough People Do." His answer was, "That sounds good, but why do you phrase it that way?" Her answer was, "I was taking notes, and those were the first words you expressed while giving the sermon."

8. *Think and Grow Rich—Napoleon Hill*

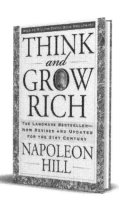

- This book is the all-time best-selling classic on business success. I have personally read and reread the book; and every time I reread it, I got new insight and inspiration, increasing my understanding of the concepts of the book.

- To me, the most important lesson in the book was when the question, "Which contribution was more important to business success, capital, management, or labor?" was discussed. The author described that each contributed equally to business success. Napoleon Hill used the example of a three-legged stool on which one leg represented capital, one leg management, and one leg labor. He explained that if you lost one of the three legs, a person would fall off the stool as quickly as the business would fall apart.

- My two partners and I have all read and reread the book from cover to cover. We all believe that the guidance that the book provides helped Success Mortgage Partners survive and then thrive through the worst recession since the depression from 2008 to 2011.

9. *The Power of Your Subconscious Mind—Dr. Joseph Murphy*

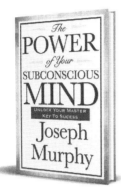

- Dr. Murphy introduced me to the depth of thought and power and creativity that you can harness through visualization and belief in an idea. He was the first author who convinced me that thoughts are actually things that just haven't manifested yet.

- Dr. Murphy taught me to believe in the concept that regardless of the odds against it, if a thought of an accomplishment can be believed, events, circumstances, opportunities, and supportive people will manifest. These additional people can bring into realization the successful outcome that was visualized through the power of the subconscious mind.

- Dr. Murphy was an ordained Protestant minister in Los Angeles, California, in the 1940s, had a vast radio audience, and was an American who fanned the flames of belief in the existence and the power of the subconscious mind.

- The book is a must read for anyone interested in this field of thought.

10. *The Secret—Rhonda Byrne*

- *The Secret* is the most recent book that I have read on the topic. Since the book was published, other similar books by different authors have also been accepted as classics on the topic. Obviously, the secret is powerful and universal. It basically explains that like attracts like and that movements throughout history frequently have been inspired by the thought, visualization, idea, and belief of one person who believes in something to such a degree that they attract like-minded people. These movements, inventions, and religious beliefs were held by individuals until other like minds were attracted to the cause, added to the pool of knowledge, and helped create advancements in medicine, art, communication, law, and so forth. In other words, advancements in civilization may have been sparked by an individual, but mass movement in any particular field intensifies when similar thoughts were embraced by a variety of people who added to the cumulative knowledge on the topic.

11. Bonus Book recently read: *Results Faster—Tony Jeary*

- In the very recent past, I have personally met Tony Jeary and become an enthusiastic student of his teachings and philosophies of life as well as his personal and business successes.

- I am happy and proud of the fact that Tony Jeary and Success Mortgage Partners have formed a permanent business relationship. It is difficult to promote an individual book of the approximately seventy-five-plus books he has authored or coauthored on principles to master personal and professional successes.

- I am currently reading one of his recent books, *RESULTS Faster!* I believe he deserves the title, "The Results Guy."

12. Bonus Book: *Never Fight with a Pig—Peter Thomas*

- This book has an interesting title and even more interesting beneficial information on the interior pages.

- His tips on negotiations of investment properties are priceless. They reflect years of his personal failures and successes in negotiating transactions.

- If you are interested in real estate investing and/ or mergers and acquisitions, read this book before you act. If you do, it will save you tons of time, worry and money. It is easy to see he is a self-made master of negotiations. The type of practical information he conveys cannot be found in a university text book or course. It is a must read!"

About the Author

Vincent Lee has been in the real estate industry for over six decades. During those sixty-plus years, Vince has worked in many facets of the real estate industry.

Starting off as a real estate salesperson, and then as a real estate appraiser trainee with the FHA, Vince then became a staff and fee appraiser for the Veteran's Administration and the FHA.

He then moved on to manage an appraisal branch for a large savings and loan. After a few years, Vince became an entrepreneur by starting his own real estate brokerage. At the same time, he became a real estate investor by purchasing residential real estate on traffic streets with rezoning possibilities. Vince was recruited and accepted an assignment as a senior vice president, regional manager, with Coldwell Banker Real Estate in Michigan. A short time later, Vince returned to real estate appraising and quickly established one of the top two largest real estate appraising firms in Michigan.

Vince is currently a principal partner in Title Partners, a large Michigan Title Agency. In addition, for the past twenty years, he has been a cofounder and partner of Success Mortgage Partners, an independent mortgage bank that has expanded from its

Michigan roots to now servicing forty-two states and the District of Columbia. He currently is the head of the Department of Sunshine and Rainbows and lives by this mantra each day.

Vince enjoys spending time with his wife, Christine. They will be celebrating their sixty-fourth wedding anniversary in a few months.

Christine and Vince have two adult children, Bridget Stockton and Owen Lee. Bridget is happily married to Don, and they have three adult children, Evan, Benjamin, and Vincent. Owen is happily married to Heather, and they have three adult children, Maura, Patrick and Declan.

ADVANCED CAREER OPPORTUNITY

- Are you supported now by your employer professionally in a career path that makes you happy?
- Are you appreciated by your existing employer?
- Does your existing employer communicate enough with you?
- With your company, are your owners, LOs, and staff happy and positive about market conditions?
- Could you benefit from the best nationally known support teachers and systems in the country?
- Could you be more successful if you realigned to SMP? We are a fast-growing independent mortgage banker with over 20 years of successful growth.
- Let us tell you about our support systems and competitive advantages.
- Why not place yourself on the SUCCESS ROAD to more income, reduced stress, and more free time.

You owe it to yourself,
CONTACT US NOW!!

If you are a loan officer go to:
www.GrowingWithKevin.com

If you are operations personnel go to:
www.SuccessMortgagePartners.com

What Success Mortgage Partners Can Do for You

The purpose of this message is to offer you an opportunity to explore coming HOME to SMP. In life, people make mistakes. That is true of loan officers, management staff, owners of independent mortgage companies, etc. Because of misunderstanding, lack of business courtesy, lack of explaining or understanding of many factors including operations, company growth, personnel, benefits, compensation, or a dozen other factors, misunderstandings frequently occur.

All individuals sometimes use negative words when positive comments should have been spoken.

Forgiveness and understanding on both sides is a virtue, not a weakness.

Frequently, with the passage of time and different market conditions, more light is shed on the misunderstanding that caused a person, on either side of the fence, to initiate a loan officer's leaving for what they perceive at the time to be a better opportunity.

Today may be the opportune time for both sides to be willing to construct a new situation to support each other's successes.

It all boils down to the question, are we better together?

If the answer to both sides is "YES," then let's just make it happen.

SUMMARY

Let's talk about new opportunities for YOU and let me explain all the NEW advantages of sharing a career with Success Mortgage Partners. Send me an email at vince@smprate.com to express your opinions, and I will respond.